DISCOVERING THE BIBLE

NOAH'S ARK

and other first Bible stories

RETOLD BY *Victoria Parker*

❖

CONSULTANT *Janet Dyson*

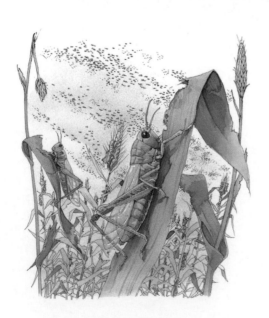

DISCOVERING THE BIBLE

NOAH'S ARK

<u>and</u> other first Bible stories

RETOLD BY *Victoria Parker* ❖ CONSULTANT *Janet Dyson*

Published by Anness Publishing Ltd,
Blaby Road, Wigston, Leicestershire LE18 4SE

Email: info@anness.com

Web: www.annesspublishing.com

Anness Publishing has a new picture agency outlet for
images for publishing, promotions or advertising.
Please visit our website www.practicalpictures.com
for more information.

Publisher: Joanna Lorenz
Editorial Director: Paula Borton
Art Director: Clare Sleven
Project Editor: Neil de Cort
Designer: Jill Mumford
Information author: Kamini Khanduri
Picture Research: Lesley Cartlidge and Libbe Mella
Copy Editor: Sarah Ridley
Indexing: Janet De Saulles
Design Consultant and cover design: Sarah Ponder
Education Consultant: Janet Dyson

Miles Kelly Publishing Limited
11 Bardfield Centre, Great Bardfield, Essex CM7 4SL

PHOTOGRAPHIC CREDITS
Page 6, (BL), Jean-Léo Dugast, Panos Pictures.
Page 13, (BL), Hutchison Library.
Page 18, (BR), Hutchison Library.
Page 27, (BL), The Stock Market.
Page 35, (BL), The Stock Market.
Page 38, (BL), The Stock Market.
Page 42, (BL), Jeremy A Horner, Hutchison Library.
Page 46, (BR), Hutchison Library.
Page 47, (BR), Hutchison Library
All other images from the Miles Kelly Archive

The Publishers would like to thank the following artists who have
contributed to this book:
Simone Boni Studio (Virgil Pomfret Agency): Vanessa Card,
Rob Sheffield, Wayne Ford, David Ashby (Illustration Ltd),
Alan Male (Linden Artists)
Maps by Martin Sanders

Contents

Introduction

The Bible is a collection of 66 books which were written over a period of nearly 1,600 years, starting from around 1400BC. Many of the stories in the Bible had been passed down from one generation to another by word of mouth and were well known for a long time before they were written down. Different books were written by different authors, and as time went by they were gradually all put together into one bigger book. This big book became the Bible. The word "Bible" comes from the Greek word "biblia", which simply means "books". The stories are all linked, together they form the story of God's relationship with his people.

As well as forming the first part of the Christian Bible, the Old Testament is also the sacred book of the Jewish people. The 39 books of the Old Testament, that tell the story of the people of ancient Israel over many centuries, appear in both the Jewish and the Christian holy texts, but in a slightly different order.

This book covers the first part of the Bible, from God's creation of the world, to the Israelites' crossing of the Red Sea. It includes the first stories of the Bible, from the Creation to the story of Adam and Eve's temptation in the Garden of Eden. This is a very important story in the Bible as it tells of the first sin in the world. It shows how Adam and Eve, even while they were still living in the Garden of Eden, disobeyed God, and were cast out of Paradise into the world.

Their two sons, Cain and Abel, were the first people born into the world, and the first people born after Adam and Eve left Eden. Cain commits a sin when he kills his younger brother Abel, and his punishment is worse than God's punishment of Adam. Cain is told he must wander the world for the rest of his life, and that the ground will no longer grow crops for him. God also puts a mark on him, to remind him of his sin, and warn other people to leave him alone. After Cain and Abel we find the story of Noah and the mighty flood, which happens because the descendants of Adam and Eve have abandoned God,

Jewish *Torah*
The book shown above is the Torah. It contains the first five books of the Old Testament that make up the Jewish religious laws. There is also a prayer shawl, and a *dreidel*, used in games played at the Hanukkah festival, the only time that the Jews can play games of chance.

and no longer live a good life. So for the only time in history God decides to wipe all life from the face of the planet. He spares only Noah and his family, who have maintained their belief in God and tried to live their lives as God wished. He seals them away, along with pairs of all the animals of the world, in the Ark that God instructed Noah to build, and He saved them from the flood.

The story called 'God's Promise to Abraham' marks the start of the most important part of the Old Testament. After the flood, Noah's descendants, just like the descendants of Adam before him, have abandoned and neglected God. Rather than destroy the world, God chooses Abraham and his descendants to become His own people, His special race on earth. The story tells how God makes an agreement, or covenant, with Abraham. If Abraham follows God's instructions, and continues to have faith in Him, Abraham's descendants will become a great people and will one day inherit the land of Canaan, called the promised land. Abraham has faith in the promise of God, and packs up his family to move to Canaan, where he settles with his family.

God's covenant with Abraham is re-established with his descendants, we see the birth of his son, Isaac, and his grandson, Jacob, and we see how God speaks to these men when they grow up, and reminds them of the promise He made to Abraham. God promised Abraham that his descendants would become a great nation, as many people as there are stars in the sky, and with Jacob we see this start to come true. Jacob fathers twelve sons who eventually become the forefathers of the twelve tribes of Israel. One son, Joseph, is sold by his brothers and taken to Egypt. The Israelites' 400 years of exile, as God told Abraham would happen, begin with Joseph's arrival in Egypt. Jacob and his family follow Joseph there to escape a terrible famine, and while they are living there, firstly as free people but later as slaves, their numbers multiply.

God said to Abraham that his descendants would live in Egypt for 400 years, and would be led to freedom and to the promised land, and we see this come miraculously true when the great leader, prophet and law-giver Moses leads the great nation to freedom across the Red Sea.

Many of the stories illustrate God testing the faith of His people. Some pass the test, like Abraham who is prepared to sacrifice his own son if it is God's will. Others, such as Cain, are weaker. But, here and throughout the whole of the Old Testament, God continues to forgive His people for their sins. He realises that the people that He created are not perfect, and is willing to accept wrong-doing from them if they remain faithful to Him and are truly sorry for their sins. Then, through His chosen leaders, He guides them to the promised land.

Wadi-Musa, Jordan
This town, on a hillside in what is now the country of Jordan, is Wadi-Musa. It lies directly on the route that the Israelites would probably have taken on their exodus from Egypt, heading north towards the promised land.

Illuminated letter
Bibles have always been regarded as very important books that contain the words of God to His people, so great care used to be taken in making the Bible look very ornate. The letter above would have taken someone a very long time to do.

Land of the Patriarchs

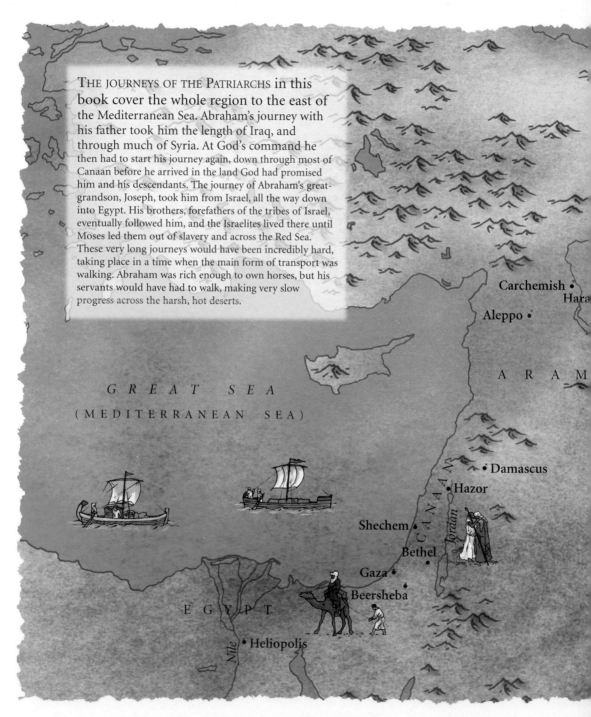

THE JOURNEYS OF THE PATRIARCHS in this book cover the whole region to the east of the Mediterranean Sea. Abraham's journey with his father took him the length of Iraq, and through much of Syria. At God's command he then had to start his journey again, down through most of Canaan before he arrived in the land God had promised him and his descendants. The journey of Abraham's great-grandson, Joseph, took him from Israel, all the way down into Egypt. His brothers, forefathers of the tribes of Israel, eventually followed him, and the Israelites lived there until Moses led them out of slavery and across the Red Sea. These very long journeys would have been incredibly hard, taking place in a time when the main form of transport was walking. Abraham was rich enough to own horses, but his servants would have had to walk, making very slow progress across the harsh, hot deserts.

Carchemish •

Hara

Aleppo •

A R A M

G R E A T   S E A

(M E D I T E R R A N E A N   S E A)

• Damascus

• Hazor

C A N A A N

Jordan

Shechem •

Bethel •

Gaza •

Beersheba

E G Y P T

Nile

• Heliopolis

Mt.Ararat

HYRCANIAN
SEA

A S S Y R I A

Mari •

Euphrates

• Accad

Tigris

• Babylon

B A B Y L O N I A

Ur

LOWER
SEA

The Creation

IN the beginning, nothing existed except God's Spirit, hovering over a darkness and never-ending water. Then God spoke. "Let there be light," He said, and suddenly there was brightness all around. God thought that the light was good, and He separated it from the darkness. He called the light Day and the dark Night. God looked on as evening drew in and watched as morning arrived. He had formed the very first day.

On the second day, God said, "Let there be skies to divide the watery wastes. Some waters will float above the skies and some will lie below." It all happened just so, and God called the skies Heaven.

Next God said, "Let all the waters under heaven be gathered into one place, so that dry land may appear. I name the waters Sea, and the dry land Earth." God looked at His work and was pleased. He commanded things to grow and at once tiny green shoots began to sprout all over the earth. As plants of all kinds took root, leafy tendrils uncurled and stretched, stems burst into bushes and trees sprang upwards. Then evening came once again and morning, making the third day.

"Let there be lights in the skies to shine on the Earth," said God. "They will mark out the passing days, months, seasons and years." He made the burning sun to rule over the day and the cooler moon to govern over the night, together with the stars. Then He set them all moving in the heavens. God was again happy with what He had done, and the fourth day came to an end.

The stars
God created the stars, along with the sun and the moon, to mark out the passing days. People have since learned how to tell the time from the sun, and mark the seasons by the movement of the stars. In the Bible, the word 'star' is used to describe any light in the sky, other than the sun and moon.

What is a day?
In the Bible, the word 'day' can mean a period of 24 hours, or an indefinite period of time. In the Creation story, everything happens in six days. Some people think this is using 'day' in its sense of 'period of time'. Others believe it is just a way of expressing God's creative energy. Finally, others believe that Creation took place in literally six days.

"Let living creatures swim in the seas and birds fly through the skies," said God, on the fifth day. Instantly, coral covered the sea beds, crabs burrowed into sand and limpets clung to rocks, shoals of fish darted through rivers and beneath waves, and sea monsters lurked in the deep. Above the Earth, flocks of birds spread their wings for the first time and began to flap and flutter, soar and swoop. And God thought it was all good work. He blessed every single creature and told them to fill the waters and the skies He had given them for their homes.

On the sixth day, God said, "Now for the living creatures of the Earth – from tiny creeping things to the largest wild beasts." He made creatures with fur, scales and hair; beasts that grunted, growled and snorted; animals

> " *And God saw everything that He had made, and behold, it was very good.* "

with claws, paws, hooves, and tails; living things that galloped and slithered. God made animals of every kind and sent them out to live in the land that He had made. He watched them and thought He had done well.

Last of all, God made people - men and women - that looked just like Him. "You shall rule over the fish of the sea and the birds of the air and the animals of the land," He told them. "You own the Earth," He said, and He blessed them. "Go and fill the whole world. I am giving the plants to you and all the living creatures for food."

As the sixth day drew to a close, God looked all around at everything He had done, and He was very pleased. The heavens and the Earth were finished, and everything had happened just as He had wished. The seventh day came and God was tired. He rested, and blessed the seventh day of the week as a holy time of rest for all people.

The animals
When God had made the land and the sea, He made the animals which lived there. The only animals named in this story are whales. Otherwise, animals are listed in very general terms. From the air come birds, from the water the fish and animals of the seas, and from the land come cattle, beasts and creeping things. These descriptions are supposed to cover all animals, from the tiniest to the most enormous, from ants to elephants.

❧ ABOUT THE STORY ❧

The Creation story tells of how the world began. In simple language, it describes the wonder of the universe, and God's power in creating it.

There is a great deal of repetition of key phrases, which mirrors the orderly way in which God created the world. The Creation story can only be understood by believing in God, not by science. The world was created by God and depends on Him for its continued existence.

The Garden of Eden

AFTER God had gathered the waters together into the sea and commanded the Earth to appear on the third day of Creation, He had been pleased with His work. But when He had looked all around Him, God had seen that the land was dry and brown. He had not yet brought rain to water the land, so nothing could grow. And besides, God had not yet created people to plough the earth, to sow crops and to care for flowers and trees.

As God thought of all these things, He sent a fine mist up from the ground. Gradually, drops of wetness drifted down and covered the face of the Earth. Then God scooped up some of the damp dust and began to shape it. Very carefully He formed a figure, until He was happy with the way it looked. Then God breathed into the figure's nostrils a deep, long breath - the breath of life. The figure blinked awake and the first Man became a living being. God looked at him with love and called him Adam.

Next, God created a special garden in a place called Eden. He ordered water to spring from the ground, and at once a river appeared. It flowed right through the garden to the edge of Eden, before bursting over the boundary and becoming four smaller rivers. The river Pishon flowed around the land of Havilah. The second river, the Gihon, circled the land of Cush. The Tigris wound its way east of Assyria. The fourth river was the mighty Euphrates.

God set about planting trees of many different kinds. All were rich with fruit, but none was more beautiful than the trees at the centre of the garden: the Tree of Eternal Life and the Tree of the Knowledge of Good and Evil.

∽ ABOUT THE STORY ∽

This is a continuation of the Creation story, dealing with God's creation of man and woman. First God creates man, then, as a companion for him, He creates woman. He gives them the Garden of Eden to live in. They can take fruit from any tree, including the Tree of Life, which will give them eternal life. The only restriction God puts upon them is to forbid them to eat from the Tree of the Knowledge of Good and Evil.

THIS SECOND DESCRIPTION OF CREATION IS WRITTEN FROM A DIFFERENT POINT OF VIEW, THIS TIME FOCUSING ON MAN. IT TALKS OF GOD SPECIFICALLY IN RELATION TO THE PEOPLE HE CREATED.∽

Adam naming the animals
God brought all the animals to Adam so he could give them names. It is possible that this was so that Adam could get to know all the different animals over which God had made him master. Adam could learn which he could keep and would work for him, like horses and sheep, cows and pigs, and which animals would run free, like the lions, tigers and bears.

God took the man He had made and placed him in Eden. "You may eat all the fruit you wish from any of my trees except the Tree of the Knowledge of Good and Evil," God warned him. "If you taste a mouthful of the fruit from that tree, you will become mortal and will one day die." Then He gave Adam His beautiful garden to care for.

God created all the animals of the earth, and all the birds that fly in the skies. He brought them to Adam to see what he would call them. One by one Adam gave them all names: the lion and the lioness, the bull and the cow, the peacock and the peahen, giraffes, zebras and antelopes . . . God ordered that from that day onwards, and ever after, every living creature on the earth should be called just as Adam had said that day.

> " *Out of the ground God made to grow every tree that is good for food.* "

God looked at each pair of animals and birds and saw that they were content together. But Adam stood alone and God realized that he was lonely. "It is not good for the man to be on his own," He thought to Himself. He sent Adam into a deep sleep, took out one of his ribs, and mended the wound. Then God tenderly shaped the rib until He was pleased with the figure He had created - the very first Woman. Then God woke Adam from his dreams and gave him his companion. Adam was delighted. "At last!" he cried. "I have something just like myself!" And Adam and Eve lived happily in God's garden of paradise.

The rivers of Eden
Of the four rivers named in this story, only the Tigris and the Euphrates are known today. There have been many attempts to identify the others as, for example, the Nile and the Indus. However no one knows for certain. The picture here shows part of the Euphrates, the largest river in western Asia.

God makes Adam
This picture shows a statue of God imagining Adam. Although it looks like Adam is looking from behind God's head, this is the sculptor's way of trying to show the picture of Adam that existed in God's mind before Adam was made, and shows how God made Adam in His own image. He formed his body from dust, just like a potter is able to make jugs from clay.

Serpent in the Garden

OF all the hundreds of creatures God had made, the snake was by far the most wily. One day he saw that Eve was going for a walk through the Garden of Eden without Adam, and he seized the chance to talk to her. "Did God tell you not to eat anything in the garden?" he asked Eve.

"We're allowed to eat any fruit except from the tree in the middle," Eve said. "God says that if we do, we will die."

"Of course you won't die!" the snake mocked. "God has told you not to eat it because it has the power to make you just like Him. You already know goodness, but when you eat from the Tree of Knowledge, you will know evil too."

Eve went to see the Tree of the Knowledge of Good and Evil for herself. How beautiful it was! Its branches were heavy with fruits. "What could be so wrong about wanting to be wiser?" she wondered. Eve reached out and plucked a plump globe. It looked and smelled so good, surely it must be delicious to eat! She took a bite, and it was the most wonderful thing she had ever tasted! Soon there was nothing left but the seeds and stalk. "I must take some to Adam," she thought, and they both ate until they were full.

Straight away, Adam and Eve realized that they had made the most dreadful mistake. Now they knew what it meant to disobey God. They suddenly felt ashamed of their nakedness and covered themselves up with fig leaves.

When Adam and Eve heard the Lord approaching they ran off. How could they face God after the terrible thing they had done? "Where are you?" the Lord asked.

Adam knew he had to tell the truth. "I heard you coming," he replied, "and I was afraid because I was naked."

Tree of Knowledge
This picture shows the Tree of the Knowledge of Good and Evil, also called the Tree of Wisdom. There are many different views as to what 'the knowledge of good and evil' might mean. One view is that it means the knowledge of right and wrong. Another is that it means the knowledge of everything in the universe. Yet another view is that the tree was just an ordinary tree, chosen by God to provide a test of man's obedience to Him.

Which fruit?
The fruit growing on the Tree of the Knowledge of Good and Evil is not named in the Bible. Most people represent it as an apple, but is more likely to be a pomegranate, like in the picture.

God roared like thunder. "Who told you that you were naked?" He demanded. "Have you eaten the forbidden fruit?"

"It was Eve who gave it to me!" Adam protested.

God turned to Eve and, with great sadness, said, "Tell me what you have done."

Eve hung her head in misery. "The snake tricked me into eating it," she cried.

Adam and Eve knew that they had filled the Lord with unhappiness and they stood before Him in utter despair.

First, God punished the snake. "You will be the most cursed of all creatures," He said. "You will crawl on your belly and eat dirt all your life."

Next God told Eve, "Childbirth will be painful, yet you will long to be with your husband and master."

> ❝ *'Cursed is the ground because of you, in toil you shall eat of it all your life.'* ❞

To Adam He said, "Because you listened to your wife rather than listening to my commands, the very ground itself will be cursed. You will work hard to grow crops, and you will need to fight weeds. After a life of hard work, you will die and return to the dust from which I made you."

Finally, God made clothes for Adam and Eve. "Now you know both good and evil, I cannot let you stay here," He explained. "If you also ate fruit from the Tree of Eternal Life, you would have to live with the pain of your shame for ever." Then God drove Adam and Eve out of Eden, and set angels with flaming swords to guard the entrance.

ADAM AND EVE, HAVE SINNED AGAINST GOD, AND THEY SUFFER BECAUSE OF THIS. THE PUNISHMENT FOR THEIR SIN IS SEPARATION FROM GOD AND EXPULSION FROM THE GARDEN, OUT INTO THE WILDERNESS. ❧

The Fall of Man

Adam and Eve's disobedience to God and their expulsion from the Garden of Eden is often called The Fall, or The Fall of Man, which represents all mankind's later sins. This picture shows Adam and Eve fleeing from the garden. Above them, an angel whirls a flaming sword and nearby stands a skeleton, symbolizing death.

❖ ABOUT THE STORY ❖

God gave Adam and Eve everything they needed to live happily together. However, they destroy the peace and innocence of the Garden of Eden by giving in to temptation and doing the one thing God has forbidden. God punishes them for their disobedience. Instead of having the eternal life God originally promised, Adam will be turned back into the dust from which he came, which means that he will eventually die.

Cain and Abel

After the Lord had thrown Adam and Eve out of paradise, in time Eve gave birth to a son. Cain was the very first baby to be born into the world, and Eve was delighted and amazed. "With the help of the Lord, I have created a new life!" she cried. Imagine her happiness later on when she had another baby – a brother for Cain, called Abel.

The two boys grew up together into strong young men. Cain chose to be a farmer and looked after the land, while Abel preferred the life of a shepherd and cared for his flock. The day came when they had to choose the best of their efforts to offer to God. Cain picked the fattest ears of corn and vegetables he had grown, while Abel took some of the first lambs that had been born in his flock. Both the men were satisfied with the fruits of their labours.

First, the Lord examined Abel's gifts and was pleased with them. But to Cain's horror, He didn't accept the older brother's presents. Cain's face fell and his heart filled with rage. What made Abel's offerings any better than his own?

The Lord said to him, "What has made you so angry? Why do you look so gloomy? You know that if you do good, I will be pleased. If you don't, sin is there waiting for you. You must always be ready to fight off evil, or it will leap at you and eat you up."

Cain should have crushed his hurt pride and made up his mind to be a better person. Instead, he found it easier to wallow in self-pity, blaming God for being unfair. Because Cain hadn't listened to the Lord's words, he didn't notice that the warning was coming true. Gradually, he

Farmers and wanderers
Cain was a farmer who works the land to grow crops. To punish him for killing Abel, God decreed that the land would no longer produce any crops for Cain, and ordered him to leave his home. This was even worse than the punishment God had imposed upon Adam, which had been to work land that was choked with weeds and thistles. Instead of living the settled existence of a farmer, Cain was condemned to a lonely life of wandering through the desert, without a home to shelter him, or a family to support him. 'Nod', the name of the faraway place Cain was banished to, means 'wandering' in Hebrew. Today, there are still tribes of wandering people, called nomads, living in desert areas of the Middle East.

Abel's sacrifice
Here, Abel has built an altar to burn his offerings to God. Later in the Bible, it becomes an offence against God if anyone other than a priest builds an altar.

grew more and more jealous of his younger brother until wickedness swallowed him, and he began to dream up plots to get Abel out of the way. One day, Cain asked his brother to go out into the fields with him. Cain found himself alone with Abel, and seizing the opportunity, he attacked his brother by surprise and killed him.

Cain was sure that no one had seen what he had done, but he was wrong. God sees everything that happens everywhere. God called to him and asked, "Cain, where is your brother, Abel?"

Cain's reply was sullen and sarcastic. "I don't know," he lied, brazenly, "I'm not my brother's keeper!"

Then the Lord accused him of his crime. "Cain! What have you done?" God was furious. "I can hear your brother's blood crying out to me from the soil where you spilled it! The very earth itself is condemning you for this terrible deed, and it will no longer grow things for you. Instead of farming your land, you must now be homeless. Go away, out of my sight, and spend the rest of your life wandering from place to place!"

Cain was devastated. "Lord! This is more than I can bear," he wept. "You, my God, are cursing me and no longer want anything to do with me. I am being sent away from the land I know and cast out among strangers. I might well die!"

"If anyone kills you," commanded the Lord, "they shall face an even more terrible punishment." He put a mark on Cain's forehead so that anyone he came across would recognize him and know to leave him alone. Then Cain was banished eastwards to a faraway place called Nod, which lay at the very edge of the world.

> 66 *And when they were in the field Cain rose up against his brother Abel, and killed him.* 99

⟡ ABOUT THE STORY ⟡

This story contains the first mention of sin. Cain is given a chance to lead a good life, but he lets jealousy get the better of him. Instead of behaving as a loving brother should, he commits a terrible crime. When God punishes him, he protests and is unrepentant. God sends him away, having first put a mark upon him. The mark serves both to protect Cain from enemies, and to remind him always of his sin.

Why did God reject Cain's offering?
In this story, no explanation is given as to why God accepts Abel's offering and rejects Cain's. However, elsewhere in the Bible, God tells Moses that all first-born animals must be sacrificed to Him (Exodus 13:2) and that the first fruits of a harvest must be offered to Him (Leviticus 23:10). The events in this story suggest that Abel was careful to make the correct offering but that Cain was not.

Noah and the Flood

IN the early days of the world, people lived much longer than they do now. Adam reached the age of 930 years old! He and Eve had many hundreds of children between them, all of whom lived for 800 years or more and who had many hundreds of children of their own. Over the centuries, each family grew. . . and grew. . . and grew. . . until men and women were everywhere throughout the world. But wickedness spread with them all over the Earth.

God watched as, one by one, people forgot about Him. He saw that they went about their own business, with no thought for anyone else, and that they carried only evil in their hearts. How it pained Him to look on the beautiful

world He had made and see that it had turned so bad! God regretted having given people life. They had spoiled everything He had so lovingly created. Very sadly, God came to a fearful decision. "I will wipe out the human race and get rid of all living creatures from the face of the Earth," He thought, " – except for Noah."

> ❝ *The Lord saw that the wickedness of man was great in the Earth.* ❞

Out of all the millions of men and women, Noah was the very last good man on the Earth – the only person who tried to live his life as God wished. Because of this, the Lord loved Noah and wanted to spare him and his family. "The world is full of evil and I am going to destroy all the people and creatures in it," God told Noah. "I am going to drown every living thing apart from you, your wife, your three sons Shem, Ham and Japheth, and their wives. Do as I tell you and you will be saved. I want you to build a huge ship out of gopher wood, 300 cubits long, 50 cubits wide and 30 cubits high and make it watertight. Shape it into an ark by covering it with a roof, put a door in the side, and give it three decks with lots of separate compartments. When the time comes, load up a male and female of every animal and bird, take plenty of food for yourselves and all the creatures, and I will shut the door."

Noah did exactly as God had told him, ignoring the people who laughed at such a seemingly ridiculous task. Then the Lord locked them all safely away. For a week they

❧ ABOUT THE STORY ❧

As time goes by, people begin to forget about God. They are no longer grateful to Him for the beautiful world He has created for them. God decides He has to destroy them all, except for Noah. Noah is the only man who lives a good life and respects God, so he is spared. God separates Noah and his family from the rest of the people by shutting them safely inside an ark. Everyone outside perishes in the flood.

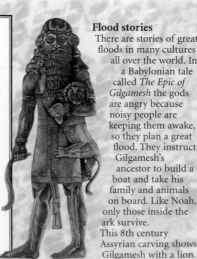

Flood stories
There are stories of great floods in many cultures all over the world. In a Babylonian tale called *The Epic of Gilgamesh* the gods are angry because noisy people are keeping them awake, so they plan a great flood. They instruct Gilgamesh's ancestor to build a boat and take his family and animals on board. Like Noah, only those inside the ark survive.
This 8th century Assyrian carving shows Gilgamesh with a lion.

Ship building
Noah and his sons would have built the ark using three layers of logs laid over each other, all coated with a sticky liquid called bitumen to make it watertight.

watched black storm clouds gather, blotting out the skies and sending dark shadows which covered the Earth. And after the seventh day, it began to rain.

> *All the fountains of the great deep burst forth, and the windows of the heavens were opened.*

It was as if fountains had burst up from the depths of the sea, while at the same time waterfalls poured down from heaven. Ponds at once became lakes; trickling streams gushed into raging torrents; swollen rivers burst their banks, swamping towns then submerging cities – and still the rain came down. People, animals and birds all fled together, higher and higher into the hills, desperately trying to find dry land on which to rest. But the waters caught them, waves tossed them, and swirling currents sucked them down. As the oceans rose, giant tidal waves crashed across whole countries, sweeping away every living thing until the Earth became a silent, underwater world. And still the rain came down. Day after day it fell, thundering down on top of the Ark. Day after long day all that Noah and his family could hear was the rain. All that they ever saw were the dark clouds and the steadily rising waters. Eventually, only the mountain tops were visible, and soon even they were hidden in the deeps.

Then there was nothing to be seen from the windows of the ark except water in every direction, stretching away as far as the eye could see, until it met the sky.

THE EPIC OF GILGAMESH MYTH IS VERY SIMILAR TO THE STORY OF NOAH. AS BOTH COULD BE DRAWN FROM MEMORIES OF AN ACTUAL EVENT IN THE SAME GENERAL AREA, THIS IS NOT AT ALL SURPRISING.

Noah's ark
The word 'ark' means 'box' or 'chest' in Hebrew. It is used here to represent a safe place provided by God. This detail from a wall painting in Saint-Savin Abbey in France shows the different decks of the ark. Noah's family and the animals are safe inside.

Wood from the trees
The Bible says that the ark is made out of gopher wood. It is not known exactly from which tree this came. This is because people studying the original texts cannot agree on how the wood named in the Bible should be translated, but it is believed it could be the cypress tree, like this one. Whichever wood was used, a huge amount was needed to make a boat the size of Noah's ark.

God's Covenant to Noah

FOR 40 days and 40 nights, it kept raining. But just when Noah and his family thought it would go on forever, it stopped. Trapped inside the ark, the people and animals fell silent and listened. The constant hammering of rain on the roof had died away.

The ark drifted helplessly on the ocean. Then they heard the noise of a great wind blowing up. It howled and wailed, gusting around the ark as God began to dry up the waters. For five months the seas very slowly sank back, until one day everyone inside the ark felt a jolt. The bottom of the ship had scraped against dry land. The ark finally grated to a halt. "At last!" thought Noah, and he peeped excitedly out of the window. But still there was nothing to see except water all around. It was many more days before he saw land. Suddenly Noah realized that the craggy points were mountains! And the ark had come to settle at the top of the very highest, Mount Ararat. But he didn't dare to open the door.

Weeks went by and everyone grew more and more impatient to leave the ark. But was it safe yet? Exactly how much land was out there? He took one of the ravens they had brought with them and released it. It flew up into the clear sky, enjoying its new freedom, but it did not return, and Noah feared it had not found land.

Noah waited until everyone could bear it no longer, and then he sent out a dove. Later the same day, it came flying wearily back to the ark. Their faces fell. The dove had not found anywhere to settle. Noah reached out his hand and gently drew the bird back into the safety of the ark.

THE DOVE HAS BECOME A SYMBOL OF PEACE THROUGHOUT THE WORLD. THIS IS WHY PEOPLE RELEASE DOVES INTO THE AIR AT INTERNATIONAL EVENTS, SUCH AS THE START OF THE OLYMPIC GAMES.

Forty days and nights
This picture shows the return of the dove. The Bible says the rains lasted 40 days and nights. Some take this literally, but some now feel that the writer just meant 'a long time.'

❧ ABOUT THE STORY ❧

By sending the flood, God took the world back to the state of chaos it was in before the Creation. When the water subsides, there is a new beginning. Noah gives thanks to God and sacrifices some of the animals to Him. God blesses Noah and promises that He will never again destroy people in another such flood. This promise is often called God's Covenant to Noah.

Another seven days passed with everyone in the ark. Then Noah again released the dove. All day long they watched the skies. As evening drew in, they caught sight of a tiny speck approaching. Closer and closer flapped the bird, until everyone could see it carried a green olive leaf in its beak. How they celebrated!

But Noah still did not let anyone go outside. He waited for another week and then set the dove free once more. This time the bird did not come back. Noah opened the door and peered into the distance. Dry ground lay wherever he looked and he heard God calling. "Noah, it's time for you and your family to leave the ark. Let all the animals go and leave them to run free across the earth."

Noah did just as he was told. After all the days of darkness on the water, everyone was so glad to feel solid ground under their feet. He built an altar and offered thanks to God. And in turn God blessed Noah, his sons and their wives, telling them to live happily together.

> ❝ *'I establish my covenant with you, that never again shall all flesh be cut off by a flood.'* ❞

"I shall never again wreak such a terrible destruction on my people and creatures - no matter how wicked the world becomes," said the Lord. "To show I will keep my word, I will set a sign in the sky. Whenever you see a band of bright colours break through the clouds, you will know that I remain true to what I have said." And God put the rainbow in the sky, to remind everyone of His promise.

Mount Ararat
This map shows one of the possible locations of Mount Ararat, near the Black Sea in what is today the country of Armenia. No one can be sure exactly where Mount Ararat is. The Bible says that 'the ark came to rest on the mountains of Ararat'. We do not know whether the Bible means on Mount Ararat itself, or in that area. People have been looking for the remains of the ark for a long time. It caused great excitement when an archaelogist claimed to have found wooden remains in Lake Kop, actually on Mount Ararat, but no one has yet been able to prove whether this is Noah's ark or not.

BLACK SEA

CASPIAN SEA

Mt. Ararat

Nineveh

MESOPOTAMIA

Tower of Babel

NOAH died at the age of 950 years old, 350 years after the flood. He lived long enough to see the birth of several generations of his family and watch them spread out into different countries all over the world.

Over time, some of Noah's thousands of descendants travelled far to the east and settled on a plain in the land of Shinar. After the families had travelled for so long, facing many hardships and dangers on the way, they were anxious to establish a proper home for themselves. They were fed up with tents and moving from place to place. Individual houses would not do; they were too easy for enemies to attack. Now that they had come so far, they weren't about to risk the chance of having to flee from their homes. Instead, the men and women decided to build a whole city where they would be protected. They could then live, work and bring up their children in comfort and safety. "And besides," they said to each other, "if we build our own city, we won't just have a wonderful home, everyone will think we're really important, too." "Yes, people are sure to come from all around to see it," they gossiped, "and won't they be jealous!"

Everyone set about the massive task of making enough bricks to build, not only the city walls, but also all the houses, shops and streets. Day after day, month after month, they baked mud into hard blocks and used tar to cement them together. Gradually, the city took shape.

Because it was all going so well, the men and women began to get carried away with their achievements. They grew proud and suggested ever grander schemes.

> **'Let us build ourselves a city, and a tower with its top in the heavens.'**

Finally one day, they hit upon the boldest plan of all. "Let's build a tower!" someone cried. "What a brilliant idea! Let's put it right in the middle of the city!" one man shouted. "We'll make it so tall that it reaches heaven," yelled another, "then we'll be nearer to God!" The people cheered and began to build.

Building the Tower of Babel
This picture shows a 17th century artist's view of how the tower would have looked in Biblical times. It shows what it would have been like building the tower in the 17th century. Here the tower is being built out of stone, when at the time the story takes place it would actually have been made of mud bricks.

The Tower of Babel
The Tower of Babel is most likely to have been a ziggurat, constructed by people in this area and also in South America as religious buildings. Remains of ziggurats have been found not only at Babel, but also Ur, Nippur, and several other places in this area.

Brick by brick, higher and higher, upwards and ever upwards, the tower rose towards the sky. Several times, the workers thought they had built it tall enough and came down to admire it. But as they stood back, craning their necks in an effort to see the top, they were always dissatisfied. "We can build higher than that," one would scoff. "Yes, I bet we could make it a little taller still," another would encourage. "I suppose the higher it is, the more everyone will admire us," another would sigh. And they'd start work all over again.

When God looked down and saw what the people were doing, He was very worried. "They are becoming so vain!" He said to Himself. "They are accomplishing a great deal, but they don't know when to stop. Soon there will be no limit to what they want. I have to do something to halt them. They could get themselves and others into terrible trouble with their foolish desires."

With one stroke, God shattered the people's over-confidence. He changed the words coming out of their mouths so that no one could communicate. Everyone found themselves listening to their friends speaking nonsense, while they each spoke a gibberish that no one else could understand. To add to everyone's annoyance, no building could be done. It was impossible for the architects to give instructions, the builders couldn't call to their workmates, and they were forced to down tools.

Eventually, the people gave up trying to talk to each other in frustration. They drifted away from the unfinished city and went off on their own to new places. And from that time onwards, people in different parts of the world have spoken different languages.

❧ ABOUT THE STORY ❧

This story shows that pride comes before a fall – God is not happy with the way the people are acting, so he changes the words they speak. This is how the Bible explains why people in different places speak different languages. This is linked to the word 'babble' which means to talk in a way that is hard to understand. We can see the link because, after God changed their words, the people could not understand each other.

Medieval scene
This detail from a medieval painting shows the building of the Tower of Babel. The men on the right are passing stones to the masons who are standing on the top of the tower, gradually adding the layers of bricks to build the tower as high as they can.

God's Promise to Abram

ONE of the descendants of Noah's son Shem was a man called Abram. Abram had grown up in Ur in Mesopotamia and married a woman called Sarai, before moving to the city of Haran with his elderly father, Terah, and his nephew, Lot. Not long after they had set up home Terah died, leaving Abram and Lot to build their lives alone.

The men worked hard, raising large numbers of sheep and cattle, and they became wealthy. Their houses were filled with beautiful possessions. They had servants to wait on them and friends for company. But Abram and Sarai did not have the one thing they wanted most – a child.

> 66 *'Go to the land that I will show you and I will make you a great nation.'* 99

Nevertheless, Abram and Lot were settled, and had no plans to move elsewhere. But one day, God spoke to Abram. "Abram, I want you to leave this place and everyone you know. Take your family, your servants, and all you own, and go where I tell you. Do as I say and you will be blessed. I will make you known as a great man, and your family will become a great people." So Abram instructed his household to pack up everything, told Lot to do the same, and they all wandered into the wilderness.

For many months the people lived in tents, moving their animals wherever the grazing seemed good. God guided them just as He had said, and brought them eventually to the country of Canaan. "Look at this land," the Lord commanded Abram. "One

day, all this will belong to your descendants." Abram built an altar and gave thanks to God. How relieved everyone was to stop travelling! The tents went up and the animals were put out to grass. At last God had shown them the place that was to be their new home.

But it wasn't long before trouble arose. Abram and Lot had so many animals that their herdsmen found the grazing areas were overcrowded. They started to quarrel over the pasture. No matter how Abram and Lot tried to solve things, there just didn't seem to be enough nearby pasture. "There's nothing for it. We'll have to split up," decided Abram. "There's ample land here for us both if we spread out. But which way will you go?"

Lot looked around him. His eyes fell on the Jordan valley, looking like the Garden of Eden. "I'll go east," he said.

It was strange after Lot and his household had gone. In the quietness, Abram again heard God calling him. "Lift up your eyes, Abram, and look all around you in every direction. All the land you see will be owned by your family forever, and you will have as many descendants as there are specks of dust on the face of the Earth. Go out and explore the countryside. I am giving it all to you."

In the days that followed, Abram grew more and more bothered about what the Lord had said. He and Sarai were still childless, and rapidly getting too old to start a family. How could God's words come true? The Lord told Abram to look up at the sky. "Do you see how many stars there are?" He asked. "Too many to count - just as it will be with your descendants. Bring me some animals and birds for sacrifice and I will show you that I mean what I say."

The following day, Abram killed some creatures for sacrifice. He cut the animals into two and placed the halves opposite each other, together with the birds, as was the custom. Then he kept watch over the offering and waited to see what would happen. As the Sun set, Abram fell into a deep sleep. He dreamt he was alone and he was terrified. Then he heard the voice of God, saying, "For 400 years your descendants will be slaves in a strange land. But

I will punish their captors and they will escape, returning to your promised land. You yourself will live for many years and will die in peace." In the pitch black of the night, Abram saw a blazing torch and a flaming fire pot pass between the sacrificed animals, and he knew that God had made a promise with him that could not be broken.

The Journey of Abram
Abram's journey started in Ur with his father, Terah. Their whole family moved to Haran, hundreds of miles to the north. Then God told Abram to move, so he set out from Haran without knowing where he was going to stop. God guided Abram to Beersheba, in Canaan. Here Abram settled, in the land that the Israelites would return to claim centuries later.

Sacrifices
The picture here shows a procession of people carrying animals to be sacrificed. In ancient times, the practice of sacrificing animals to God was commonplace. Sometimes this was done to honour God, or give thanks. At other times, it was to make amends for some wrong-doing.

> ❖ **ABOUT THE STORY** ❖
>
> *God tells Abram that his descendants will become a great people and that the land of Canaan will belong to them. Abram is unsure as he has no children, but he sees a sign from God, he hears God's voice and no longer has any doubts.*

Promise of a Son

AFTER God had made His covenant with Abram, he and his wife couldn't wait for the time when they would have a child. But the days passed into months, the months turned into years, the years stretched into decades, and there was no sign that Sarai would have a baby. As the couple grew older, their hope turned into impatience and frustration. "Take my maid Hagar as a second wife," Sarai told Abram, at her wits' end. "God might let her have children for you."

As soon as Hagar realized that she was pregnant, she began to put on airs and graces and look down on Sarai. "I have succeeded where you failed," she told her former mistress, "so I must be better than you." She started to order Sarai about, becoming more and more rude to her, until one day Sarai had had enough. She punished Hagar so severely that she ran into the desert.

An angel found Hagar weeping by a spring. "What are you doing here?" he asked. "God wants you to return to your mistress and behave yourself better. You will soon give birth to Abram's son and he will grow up to be a mighty ruler. The Lord wants you to call him Ishmael." And Hagar did just as the angel told her.

Years went by and Abram turned 99 years old. Just as he and Sarai had given up hope of ever having children together, the Lord spoke to him once more. "I am God Almighty and I will keep my covenant to you. I tell you again, your descendants will be kings who will rule over Canaan. I want you to change your name to Abraham, and I want Sarai to become Sarah."

> 66 *'Behold, you are with child, and shall bear a son; you shall call his name Ishmael.'* 99

"How can a child be born to a man who is nearly 100 years old and a woman who is 90?" the cowering Abraham protested. "And what about my son, Ishmael?"

∽ ABOUT THE STORY ∽

Because of his faith, Abraham is prepared to wait patiently until God gives him the child He promised. Sarah, on the other hand, grows more desperate the older she gets. Unable to wait any longer and doubtful as to whether God will ever fulfil His promise, she suggests that Abraham has a child with Hagar. But Ishmael is not the son God promised to Abraham, and Sarah is not happy until she has a son of her own.

Old oak tree
People used to like sitting under oak trees because of the shade of its leaves. Big oak trees standing alone were also often used as landmarks for travellers.

Annunciation
When the angel appeared to Hagar in the desert, this was an annunciation. The word 'annunciation' means proclamation, or announcement.

God thundered, "Ishmael will be the leader of a great nation. But this time next year, Sarah will have a son of her own, whom you must call Isaac."

Some weeks later, Abraham was sitting and wondering about the Lord's words, when he saw three strangers approaching. Abraham knew they were messengers from God and he rushed to his nearby tent for food and drink while the men cooled off under a broad oak tree.

"God will visit you next spring and Sarah will have a son," the men told Abraham, as they refreshed themselves. Abraham didn't realize that Sarah was listening at the tent door and could hear everything. "How can we have a baby now?" she scoffed out loud. "We're both far too old!"

"Nothing is too difficult for the Lord," the strangers insisted, and they went on their way, leaving the couple quite bewildered.

At last the time came when God fulfilled His vow. On a beautiful spring day Sarah gave birth to a son whom they called Isaac – all just as the Lord had said.

"God has made me so happy!" sang Sarah. "No one who hears of this can fail to be happy too!"

But despite the celebrations, Abraham was saddened. Now Sarah had had a child of her own, she wanted to get rid of Ishmael and his mother. Abraham loved each of the boys and hated the thought of losing Ishmael. God reassured him. "Don't worry, do as Sarah says," He told Abraham. "I will make both of your sons the founders of great peoples."

The next morning, before anyone else was awake, Abraham said a last and sad goodbye to Hagar and Ishmael and sent them off into the desert. They walked and walked through the heat and the dust until they were exhausted, and the supplies of food and water that they had brought with them were all gone . There was no sign of life in any direction and Hagar knew that they were going to die. She couldn't bear to watch Ishmael suffer, so she laid him down under a shady bush and wandered a little way off before collapsing with grief. But God heard Hagar weeping and He sent an angel to comfort her. "Have no fear," said the angel. "Ishmael will not die. God has promised that he will grow to be a great man. Now go and take care of him." Summoning all her remaining strength, Hagar picked herself up. To her surprise, she saw a spring a little way off and she dashed to get water to revive her son. Hagar and her son lived together in the wilderness for a long time and Ishmael grew up to be a brave warrior, the father of all the Arab peoples.

Living in tents
Today, some people live a nomadic lifestyle in the deserts of the Middle East, as Abraham did. They keep herds of animals and follow them around wherever there is good grazing. Abraham, though, was used to living in one place, so would not have been as used to this life as these Bedouin people.

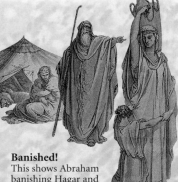

Banished!
This shows Abraham banishing Hagar and Ishmael. Abraham does not want to lose Ishmael, and wishes that God would recognize both his sons. Abraham always accepts God's will, but his love for Ishmael causes him to question God on this occasion.

Arabs
Abraham's first son, Ishmael, grew up to be a great warrior. While Isaac was the father of the Israelite nation, Ishmael grew up to become the ancestor of all the Arab people.

Abraham and Isaac

AFTER the many years of waiting, Abraham and Sarah's happiness was complete. Isaac grew to be a lively, strong little boy. As his parents watched him run errands and play in the fields with the other children, it was hard for them to believe that their son was a part of the Lord's great plan.

Then one day, Abraham heard God calling him once again. "Abraham! Take your only son, Isaac – who I know you love dearly – and go to a mountain I will show you. There, I want you to offer him to me as a sacrifice."

Abraham was truly horrified. How could God be asking him to kill his own son? The Lord knew how long

Abraham and Sarah had been desperate for children, and how precious their son Isaac was! What could Abraham say to Sarah? And how on earth could he tell Isaac?

Abraham mentioned nothing to his family of God's terrible request. The next morning, he rose early and took his son and two servants to cut firewood, which they loaded on to a donkey. The awful secret Abraham carried was far heavier. They set off across the countryside, Abraham hanging his head in misery. After three days, Abraham knew they had reached God's chosen place.

❧ ABOUT THE STORY ❧

Although Abraham is horrified at the idea of killing his son, he puts his faith in God and obeys Him. He follows God's instructions until the point where he is about to make the sacrifice. When God is certain that Abraham's faith is strong, He spares the boy and repeats His promise, that Abraham's descendants will become a great people. By proving that he puts God above all, Abraham has passed the test God set for him.

Climbing the mountain
God would not usually ask anyone to make a child sacrifice. It seems clear, though, that God never actually intended Abraham to sacrifice his son.

Dome of the Rock
The Bible describes the sacrifice as taking place on a mountain in the land of Moriah. This is believed to be the hill in Jerusalem where King Solomon later built his magnificent temple. Later still, in the 7th century AD, the Muslims conquered Jerusalem and built a mosque where the temple had stood. This mosque, called the Dome of the Rock, still stands today.

"Stay here with the donkey and wait for us," he told the servants. "Isaac and I are going to go and make an offering to God." Then Abraham and Isaac began to climb the steep hillside.

After a while, Isaac grew a little puzzled. "Father," he asked. "I'm carrying the wood, you have a knife and some fire, but where is the lamb we're going to offer?"

Abraham tried hard to keep his voice steady. "My son," he replied with great anguish, "God will provide Himself with a lamb."

Side by side, the two went on until they reached the spot for the sacrifice. They gathered stones and built an altar. Then, Abraham arranged the firewood. The time had come. Tenderly, Abraham bound Isaac and lifted him on to the sacrificial pile. He stretched out his hand for the knife. Overcome by grief, Abraham steeled himself to obey God. He raised the blade up over the terrified boy.

All at once he heard someone calling his name. "Abraham! Abraham!"

Abraham stopped still. Slowly, he lowered the knife and listened. Then he fell to his knees. It was the voice of the Angel of the Lord.

"Here I am," Abraham replied.

"Abraham!" called the Angel of the Lord. "Do not harm the boy! Since you would have given God your only son, He knows now that you are true to Him."

Abraham could hardly believe his ears. Slowly, he raised his eyes to look at the trembling, terrified boy tied to the altar. His son had been spared! There was some movement in a thicket and Abraham caught sight of a ram, snared in the brambles and struggling to break free. Weeping with

" *'Because you have not withheld your son I will multiply your descendants'* **"**

joy, Abraham lifted Isaac down from the firewood. He took the animal and offered it in Isaac's place, giving great thanks to God. And the Angel of the Lord called to Abraham for a second time from Heaven. "Abraham, the Lord says that because you have obeyed Him, both you and your son shall be blessed. You will have as many descendants as there are stars in the sky, as many descendants as there are grains of sand on the seashore, and they shall become a great people."

Abraham and Isaac
God knew where he planned to put Abraham's faith to the test, but it was not near Abraham's house. It took Abraham and Isaac three days to make the journey from their home in Beersheba to Mount Moriah, at the other end of the Salt Sea. It must have been a terrible journey for Abraham, giving him a long time to reflect on what he knew God had asked him to do. Even after this gruelling journey, Abraham was still faithful to God, and would have sacrificed his only son had God demanded it.

Isaac and Rebekah

THE years passed and Abraham outlived Sarah, reaching an extremely old age, just as God had told him he would. The most important thing to the elderly man was seeing their son, Isaac, settled with a wife before he died. Abraham had to be sure that Isaac would carry on the family, so God's promise that his descendants would become a great nation could be fulfilled. He called his most trusted servant to him and said, "Go back to my country of Mesopotamia, where I grew up all those years ago. Find Isaac a good woman from my own family to be his wife." Honoured to be entrusted with such an important task, the servant loaded up ten camels with lots of expensive gifts of jewellery, perfume and silks and set off on the difficult trek across the desert.

Abraham's servant was tired and dusty when he eventually reached the city of Nahor and he made straight for the waterhole. Dusk was falling and the women were coming to draw their water for the night. "Maybe I'll find one among them fit to be Isaac's wife," the servant thought to himself. "Oh God," he prayed silently, "please help me pick the right girl. Show me which one I should choose and give me a sign so that I can be sure. I'll ask the girl to give me a drink from her water jug, and if she says yes and offers to fetch me some water for the camels too, I'll know she's the one Isaac should marry."

> ❝ *Before he had done speaking, behold Rebekah came out with her water jar upon her shoulder.* ❞

While Abraham's servant was still deep in prayer, a beautiful young girl made her way up to the well. She lowered her jug down into the depths and drew it up again, heavy with water. There was something about the girl that caught the servant's attention. "But surely the very first young woman couldn't be the one?" he wondered. Hurrying up to her, he asked, "May I have a little of your water to drink?"

"Of course," she answered with a smile, and poured him some straight away. She watched as the servant refreshed himself and then laughed, "Your camels look as if they could do with a drink, too." She went off to water the thirsty animals. Abraham's servant was so surprised that he nearly forgot why he was there. Luckily, he remembered in time and rushed to offer her some of the gold jewellery he had brought as presents.

He asked the girl who she was, and could hardly believe it when the girl replied, "I am Rebekah, daughter of Bethuel." Bethuel was Abraham's nephew! He thanked God for guiding him straight to his master's relatives.

The servant accompanied Rebekah back home and her brother, Laban, hurried to make his guest welcome, stabling the camels and setting out a feast. But the servant couldn't bring himself to eat anything until he knew whether or not Rebekah would agree to be Isaac's wife. After he'd explained everything, Laban and Bethuel, Rebekah's father, agreed it could only be God's work. "We must do as He wishes," they told Abraham's servant, "Rebekah shall go with you to marry Isaac." Before the celebrations began, the servant shared out Abraham's presents: more gold and silver jewellery for Rebekah, together with richly embroidered materials; valuable trinkets and ornaments for the rest of the family. They feasted until late into the night and the following morning, Rebekah left for the long trip to her new home.

It was late one evening when Isaac looked up and saw the tiny shapes of camels approaching in the distance. Suddenly nervous and not knowing quite what to expect, he slowly began to walk out to meet them.

"Who's that?" Rebekah asked the servant, as she caught sight of the broad-shouldered young man walking hesitantly towards them.

"He's your husband," came the reply, to Rebekah's delight. Abraham's servant explained to Isaac everything that had happened, how God had made sure that Isaac and Rebekah would be together, and Isaac welcomed Rebekah as his wife with love in his heart.

The Tribes of Israel

Isaac's grandsons were to become the fathers of the twelve tribes of Israel. When the Israelites reached the promised land, each tribe was promised an area that they could call their own, but they could only claim the areas that were allotted to them once they had defeated the people that were already there. The Israelite tribe of Dan, in the north, originally lived around the city of Beth-dagon, but they could not defeat the Philistines and force them to leave, so they had to move to a new area.

Abraham's gifts
The gift a bridegroom gives to his bride's family is called a dowry, given as compensation for the loss of a daughter. It might include jewellery like this, necklaces, rings, earrings and nose rings.

Water carrier
Rebekah may have been carrying a water pot like this when she met Abraham's servant.

❧ ABOUT THE STORY ❧

It is important that Isaac marries, so he can have children and fulfil God's promise. Abraham's servant prays to God to help him find the right girl. Rebekah appears, as if in answer to his prayer. Rebekah's family agree to the wedding, knowing it to be God's will.

Jacob and Esau

GOD blessed Isaac and Rebekah with twins. But when the babies were born, it was strange to see that they looked nothing like each other. Esau, the elder, was covered with red hair, and Jacob, the younger, was smooth-skinned. The parents loved both children, but as time went by and the boys grew up, each secretly grew to have a favourite. Isaac became particularly fond of Esau, because he proved to be good at hunting and Isaac's favourite meal was venison. Rebekah, though, grew to love Jacob best,

> **Then Jacob gave Esau bread and pottage of lentils and he ate and drank. Thus Esau despised his birthright.**

because he didn't like running about outdoors and preferred to stay quietly at home with her.

Because of their different characters, Esau and Jacob were often to be found arguing - especially over Esau's birthright. Even though Esau was only minutes older than Jacob, as the first-born, he was the heir to all Isaac's riches and would become head of the family when their aging father died. But one day, Jacob saw an opportunity to seize the precious birthright for himself. He was cooking some lentil soup when Esau returned home from a long hunting trip, faint with hunger. "Give me some of that, I'm famished!" his brother demanded.

Jacob was angry at his rudeness. "I'll swap you some soup for your birthright," he bargained.

Esau didn't even think about what he was doing. "All right. It won't be any good to me if I've died of starvation," he snapped, tormented by the good smell.

"Swear you mean it," said Jacob solemnly, holding the steaming bowl just out of Esau's reach.

"I swear on my life that I give you my birthright!" yelled Esau. "Now hand me the soup before I collapse!" In a few gulps, it was all gone.

Years went by and Isaac became old and blind. He knew that he didn't have long to live and he called Esau to him. "My best son," he said, tenderly. "Go and hunt a deer so I may taste the venison you cook for me just one more time. Hurry, so I can give you my blessing before I die."

But Rebekah had overheard. She was well aware that if a man on his deathbed blessed or cursed someone, it sealed their future either good or bad. She was determined that Isaac should bless Jacob instead of Esau, and dashed off to

Wild goats
Esau would have hunted animals such as the ibex, a type of wild goat. Ibexes are still found in rocky areas of the Middle East today. He would have used weapons similar to those that some hunters use today such as traps and nets, as well as a bow and arrows.

Old age
Isaac was already over a hundred when he blessed the wrong one of his sons, but he lived on until the age of 180. Many people in the Bible lived to extraordinary ages, for example Abraham lived to 175, Adam to 930 and Noah to 950. The oldest man in the Bible is Noah's grandfather, Methuselah, who lived until he was 969. Old people were held in great respect for their experience and wisdom.

The birthright
A father's special blessing to his oldest son, normally just before he died, was called the birthright. It gave the son leadership over his brothers, but it also placed on him the responsibility of taking care of the family after his father's death. While it most often went to the eldest son, a father could choose to give it to a younger son, or to someone else. A birthright could be sold, or given away before it was passed on by the blessing, but once the special blessing had been given, it could not be taken back. This is why fathers usually waited until they thought they were soon to die before passing on the birthright.
Esau would have known how important the birthright was, and the fact that he gave it away so easily shows that he did not deserve to receive his father's blessing.

clothes, covered his hands, face and neck with the hairy goat skins, and sent him in to see Isaac.

"Father, it's me, Esau," lied Jacob.

Isaac was surprised. "That was quick!" he said.

"God helped me in my hunting," Jacob replied. Isaac was suspicious, but feeling Jacob's hairy skin reassured him. He ate the food, kissed his son, and blessed him with every good wish. "God will make you rich and prosperous, a ruler of great men, and master over this family. May God reward everyone who blesses you and curse everyone who wishes you bad luck!"

Scarcely minutes after Jacob had left, Esau arrived. "Here we are, father," he said. "Enjoy the delicious meal I have brought you and then you can bless me."

Isaac began to tremble. "Who are you?" he asked.

"Don't you recognize your first-born son?" Esau laughed. "It's me, Esau."

Isaac was pierced with anguish. "But I've already blessed somebody else and I can't take it back!"

Esau was devastated. "Father, bless me too!" he begged.

"I can't, my son," the grief-stricken Isaac told him. "I've blessed your brother with everything. He will become rich, a ruler of men and master of the family."

The tears streamed down Esau's face and Isaac blessed him as best he could. "Your life will be difficult, but you will become a great warrior and a great leader, and you will break away from your brother's control."

From that day on, Esau hated Jacob bitterly and plotted how he might kill him. But just in time, Rebekah sent Jacob away to live with her brother in Haran, so he would be safe from harm.

find him. "Be quick," she instructed Jacob. "Go and get two young goats so I can cook them up into a tasty meal for you to take to your father. He'll think you're Esau and will give you his final blessing."

"But Esau is much more hairy than me," Jacob objected. "If father realizes that I'm trying to trick him, he will probably curse me instead of blessing me."

"Leave that to me," Rebekah replied, so Jacob did what he was told. Then his mother dressed him in Esau's best

---

❖ ABOUT THE STORY ❖

Part of the birthright Isaac will pass down to his son is God's promise to Abraham, that his descendants will be a great people and that the land of Canaan will one day be theirs. Although Jacob deceives his father in order to receive the birthright, the blessing is still valid. Rebekah suffers for her role in the deception because her favourite son is forced to run away from home.

The Journey of Jacob

Jacob's journey from Beersheba to his mother's family in Haran is a long one. On the way to meet Laban, Jacob saw his vision of the angels travelling up and down a stairway to heaven. He renamed the place at which he saw this vision Bethel, which means 'house of God'. When he returns after 20 years away, he meets his brother Esau by the river Jabbok, at a place called Penuel.

Jacob's Ladder

JACOB'S path to safety lay across the desert. The journey was so tough that at times he'd wonder if it wouldn't have been better to stay and face Esau's anger. By day he'd roast as the sun baked down, while at night he'd shiver out in the open under the stars. At least he didn't find it difficult to sleep – even though he had only rocks for pillows. At the end of each day, he'd gratefully collapse with exhaustion and fall asleep at once.

> *He dreamed that there was a ladder and the top of it reached to heaven.*

One night Jacob had a vivid dream that there was a huge staircase stretching all the way from the earth to heaven. Angels were going up and down between the two, and at the very top of the stairs stood God Himself. The Lord spoke to Jacob and repeated the promise He had made to Abraham. "Your descendants will become a great people," He said. "No matter where you go, I will keep you safe and bring you back home to this land."

As soon as Jacob woke, he took the large, flat stone that had been under his head and stood it upright in the ground to mark where he had been lying. He anointed it with oil in a sacred ritual and named the spot Bethel, or God's house. Then he prayed that God would keep His word and be with him on his journey, before continuing on his way.

Angels
The word 'angel' means messenger. In the Bible, angels are the messengers of God. They appear in front of people to tell them God's commands, or to inform them of something God wants them to know. The phrase 'the angel of the Lord' is used to describe how God came to people in human form, to give them a special message.

ABOUT THE STORY

While Jacob is dreaming, God appears to him, standing at the top of a huge staircase often called 'Jacob's ladder'. God repeats the promise He made to Abraham, which He renewed with Jacob's father Isaac – that Jacob's descendants will become a great people and will inherit the land of Canaan.
Jacob asks God to protect him on his journey across the desert and promises to serve Him if he does so.

Jacob and Rachel

As Jacob drew near to Haran, he came to a field where shepherds were watering their flocks at a well. He spoke to them, hoping they could give him directions, "My brothers, where do you come from?"

They said, "We are from Haran." Jacob knew that this was very close to where Laban lived.

"Do you know Laban of Nahor?" Jacob asked them.

"Yes, we know him well," they replied. One of the men pointed across the pasture at a shepherdess approaching with her sheep. "That's his daughter, Rachel," he said

Jacob waited patiently until his cousin had driven her flock up to the well. He watched as she began trying to roll away the heavy stone that covered the well mouth and leaped up to help. "I'm Jacob," he told her, to her great surprise. "I'm your Aunt Rebekah's son." And he greeted her properly with a kiss. With great excitement, Rachel ran off to tell her father that his nephew was here.

> ❝ *Then Jacob kissed Rachel and wept aloud. And Jacob told Rachel that he was her father's kinsman.* ❞

Just as Laban had rushed to welcome Abraham's servant so many years before, he now hurried out to meet Abraham's grandson. Laban greeted Jacob as if he were his long-lost son and took him home, where Jacob explained everything to him.

A S ABRAHAM'S SERVANT HAD FOUND HIS MASTER'S FAMILY, SO JACOB IMMEDIATELY FINDS HIS MOTHER'S FAMILY AND HIS FUTURE WIFE. GOD IS ALWAYS PRESENT, MAKING SURE THAT EVERYTHING HAPPENS ACCORDING TO THE WAY THAT GOD HAS PLANNED IT. ↶

Women in the Bible
Women in ancient times played an important part in daily life. Probably their most significant role was that of mother. A mother was honoured, feared and obeyed in her household. She was responsible for naming her children, and for their early education. They went to worship at religious gatherings and brought offerings for sacrifice. If there were no male heirs, a woman could inherit land and property from her parents.

↠ ABOUT THE STORY ↞
This story tells of the beginning of Jacob's love for Rachel, one of the Bible's outstanding examples of human love. Rachel is described as a woman of great beauty and Jacob falls in love with her as soon as he lays eyes upon her. His love remains strong until the day Rachel dies. Rachel is important as her sons are the ancestors of three of the tribes of Israel: Benjamin, Ephraim and Manasseh.

The Wedding of Jacob

LABAN welcomed Jacob to live with him and the grateful young man tried to show his thanks by working in his uncle's fields, shepherding his flocks. After four weeks had gone by, Laban called Jacob to him. "It isn't fair that you should work for me for nothing," he said, generously. "What can I give you as payment?" Jacob didn't need to think about it. Over the past month he had fallen deeply in love with Rachel and wanted to marry her. Rachel was young and full of life, and her beauty made her elder sister, Leah, seem plain and dull in comparison.

> ❝ *'I will serve you seven years for your younger daughter Rachel.'* ❞

"I will work for you for nothing for seven years if you promise to let me marry Rachel," Jacob told his uncle. "I'd rather give her to you than anyone else," the delighted Laban replied. So Jacob remained working for his uncle and the seven years flew past as if they were only seven days. At last the wedding day arrived and Laban threw a great feast. He invited all his friends and neighbours from miles around and they celebrated well into the evening. Then Laban covered his daughter's face with her wedding veil and sent her to Jacob's tent.

Next morning, Jacob was horrified to find that it was Leah, not Rachel, who was lying by his side. He woke Laban in a fury. "You've tricked me into marrying the

M OSES WOULD LATER FORBID A MAN FROM MARRYING HIS WIFE'S SISTER DURING HIS WIFE'S LIFETIME. THE TENSION BETWEEN JACOB AND HIS WIVES SHOWS THE WISDOM OF THE LAWS GOD GAVE TO MOSES

Wearing a veil
Jacob could not tell which sister he was marrying because Leah's face was hidden by her veil. The tradition of brides wearing veils continues in many cultures today, though often the face is only partly covered. In some Middle Eastern countries the women wear veils all the time, not just at their weddings.

Powerful plant
In ancient times, people believed that the root of the mandrake plant had the power to increase wealth and overcome infertility. Women who were unable to have children used to go in search of mandrakes. Although Jacob loved Rachel, it was Leah and the maids who gave him the children he wanted first.

wrong sister!" he yelled at the top of his voice. "I didn't work for you for seven years to have Leah for my wife!"

Quite calmly, his uncle replied, "In this country, it's not the done thing for the younger daughter to take a husband if her older sister is still single. Now that Leah is a married woman, I'm more than happy to give you Rachel too – in return for another seven years' work, of course. Also, you must wait until the week of Leah's wedding festivities is over before marrying her."

There was nothing Jacob could do and because he loved Rachel so much, he agreed to his uncle's demands. At the end of the week, he and Rachel were finally allowed to be together, and Jacob began seven years more work.

As soon as Jacob and Rachel were married, poor Leah found herself left out and ignored. God saw how rejected and miserable she felt and He took pity on her, blessing her with a baby boy. Leah went on to have three more of Jacob's sons while Rachel remained childless. "Jacob, I shall die if we can't have a baby!" she wept one day.

Her husband was just as frustrated. "What can I do about it? It's all up to God," Jacob yelled back.

"Then marry my maid, Bilhah," Rachel cried. "If she has children, they'll count as mine."

Bilhah gave birth to two sons. But, no matter how hard she tried, Rachel couldn't stop hoping for children of her own. God kept her waiting a long time before He granted her wish. Even after Leah's maid, Zilpah, bore Jacob two sons, and Leah herself had a further two boys and a daughter, Rachel remained childless. Finally, God took pity on her, and He sent Rachel a little boy. She was overjoyed and treasured her son, calling him Joseph.

Wine sets
At Jacob's wedding feast, wine would have been served with the food. Wealthy people had bronze wine sets made up of three pieces: a juglet to scoop the wine out of a storage jar, a strainer to filter out any impurities, and a shallow bowl to drink from.

❖ ABOUT THE STORY ❖

Jacob deceived his brother, Esau, out of his birthright. Now it is his turn to be deceived by his uncle. Although Jacob has already worked for Laban for seven years before the wedding, he is tricked into marrying the wrong sister, and forced to work another seven years in order to marry Rachel. Jacob has God's blessing, though, and he fathers twelve sons, who go on to be the forefathers of the twelve tribes of Israel.

Jacob's Return

JACOB endured the further seven years' work he had agreed to do for Laban in return for Rachel's hand in marriage. But he planned to leave his cheating uncle as soon as the time was up. When that day arrived, Laban was horrified. "You're the only reason I've become so wealthy," he told Jacob. "God must truly be with you, because everything you turn your hand to is a success. What can I do to make you change your mind?" Jacob saw the chance to start building a flock of his own and told his uncle that he would only stay if Laban would let him have any sheep or goats that had spotted or black coats. Laban readily agreed, secretly thinking he would trick Jacob once again. He told his sons to sort out all the non-white animals and hide them in pastures far away. But God helped Jacob outwit his uncle. He blessed the remaining flocks so that some lambs and kids were born with spotted and black coats. Slowly, Jacob separated out a flock, and at the end of six years, he was a rich man.

As Laban and his sons grew more and more jealous at how well Jacob had done for himself, living with his uncle became increasingly unpleasant for Jacob. He prayed to God for guidance and decided that it would be best to return home. Jacob knew that Laban would be very angry at losing not only his daughters but also his best shepherd and would make it extremely difficult for him to leave. So he didn't tell his uncle he was going. He waited until sheep-shearing time, when Laban and his sons had to stay away in the fields, then he fled with his wives, children, servants, flocks and possessions.

When Laban found out, he dashed off in pursuit. After a week's hard riding, he caught up with Jacob and the two men had a bitter argument. Laban accused Jacob of stealing his daughters and his animals, while Jacob reminded Laban that he had deliberately deceived him more than once. No doubt things would have come to blows, but God had warned Laban in a dream not to harm Jacob in any way. Eventually, when neither man would apologize, they agreed to make up for the sake of Jacob's children, and they went their separate ways in peace.

Now Jacob's main worry was his brother. While he hoped that Esau had had a change of heart during the 20 years they had been separated, Jacob feared the worst. He remembered the deep hatred there had been between them, and Jacob suspected that Esau was still determined to kill him. In an effort to patch things up, Jacob sent messengers on ahead with gifts. But just in case his brother wasn't prepared to forgive him, Jacob split his household up into two groups. Then if Esau attacked the family group, Jacob could be sure that at least some of them stood a good chance of escaping.

Meeting place
When Jacob and Esau met again after 20 years the meeting took place where the river Jabbok flows into the river Jordan, above, to the north of the Dead Sea. Today, the Jabbok is known as the river Zerqa.

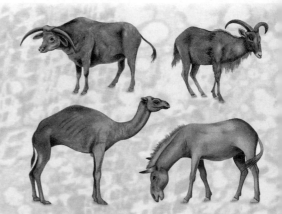

Sending gifts
It was common practice for two people to send gifts to each other before meeting. The gifts were usually related to the people's occupations, so Jacob, as a herdsman, sent livestock like sheep, goats and camels to Esau.

As they drew close to their journey's end Jacob became more and more troubled. One evening he took himself off to find a quiet place where he could think. Though Jacob was sure he was alone, a stranger appeared from out of the darkness and challenged him to wrestle. They struggled all night long, equally matched in strength and will, and neither grew any nearer to winning. When dawn began to break the two men broke apart, worn out. "What's your name?" asked the stranger.

"Jacob," came the weary reply.

"From now on you will be known as Israel," the stranger commanded, vanishing as suddenly as he had appeared. Jacob was left on his knees in awe. His new name meant 'he who has grappled with the Lord', and he realized he had been fighting with God Himself. After having cheated to become Isaac's heir and having been sent away from the land the Lord had especially chosen for Abraham, Jacob had proved his

> 66 *So Jacob called the place Penuel, saying 'For I have seen God face to face.'* 99

worth and God had blessed him with a new beginning.

Then Jacob went down to meet Esau, who had come with 400 men at the ready. Telling his family to stay back, Jacob nervously walked to his brother. Jacob left God to decide his fate and bowed down before his brother. To his complete amazement, Esau ran to meet him. "Welcome home!" he cried, throwing his arms around Jacob, and the brothers both wept with happiness.

Dreams from God
Dreams are used in the Bible as a means by which God can send messages to the sleeper. God's warning to Laban is an example of such a dream.

Jacob's prayer
Jacob prays to God that Esau will not harm him or his family, and trusts in God to keep them all safe.

> ❧ **ABOUT THE STORY** ❧
>
> *When Jacob is near Canaan, just before he is reunited with his brother, he wrestles with a stranger, who turns out to be God Himself. This is the culmination of a lifetime's struggle for Jacob. He is unlike Abraham and Isaac, in that his faith did not come easily to him. In the end, though, he has proved his worth and God blesses him with a new name and a new beginning.*

Joseph and his Brothers

JACOB settled in the land of Canaan with his large family: his four wives had had many children between them. Just like his father, Isaac, Jacob had a favourite child – Joseph, the son of his beloved wife Rachel. When the boy reached 17 years old, Jacob gave him a special present: a beautiful long-sleeved coat, elaborately woven in many different colours and patterns. His 11 brothers knew that the expensive gift showed Jacob thought of Joseph as his heir – despite the fact that he wasn't the eldest – and they were extremely jealous. Their resentment and hatred grew when Joseph described two dreams he had had. "First I saw us all working in the fields, tying up sheaves of corn," he told them. "But all of a sudden, your sheaves turned to mine and bowed to it! And my second dream was even more peculiar. This time it was the Sun, the Moon and 11 stars that all bowed down to me!"

His brothers were immensely annoyed. "So are you saying that you're going to rule over us?" they mocked, sarcastically. Even his father was irritated.

"Do you really want us and your mother to come and grovel at your feet?" Jacob snapped. But all the same, he couldn't put his son's words out of his mind.

It was usual for the brothers to ignore Joseph as far as they could and they often sneaked off together, taking their flocks over the fields without him. Jacob would send Joseph after them to report back on what they were up to – which only made the brothers dislike him even more. One day the 11 boys had travelled to the very furthest pastures, thinking they had left Joseph behind as usual, when they noticed a bright-coated figure in the distance, heading their way. "It's the dreamer," groaned one.

"Coming to spy on us again," sneered another.

"Wait a minute," interrupted a third. "This could be the chance we've been waiting for. We're a long way from home and there's no one around. Why don't we do away with him?" The others soon took up the idea.

"We could kill him and hide the body where no one will find it," said one. "And we could tell Father that a wild animal attacked him," suggested another. They were enjoying laying their plans but Reuben, the eldest, was shocked. Thinking quickly, he

> **"** *They said, 'Here comes this dreamer. Come now, let us kill him.'* **"**

came up with a way to stop them. "I say we don't kill Joseph," he urged. "Do any of you really want to be responsible for his death? Why don't we dump him in a pit?" The brothers reluctantly agreed. Little did they know that Reuben intended to come back and rescue Joseph.

When the boy reached his brothers they suddenly turned on him and attacked him, kicking him to the ground. Enraged by the sight of the coat, they ripped it off and stamped on it in the dirt, before throwing their bruised and bleeding brother into a disused well. All except Reuben were well satisfied with their work and while the upset Reuben wandered off, out of earshot of Joseph's cries for help, the others sat down to eat.

Halfway through the meal the brothers were startled to hear people approaching. Nervously, they looked up and saw a band of Ishmaelite traders coming towards them, their camels loaded down with exotic spices. Judah's eyes lit up. "Here's a way to make ourselves some money and solve the problem of what to do with Joseph at the same time," he told his brothers, cunningly. "These merchants are on their way to Egypt. I'm sure they'd be glad to have a slave to sell when they get there." And the boys took 20 pieces of silver in exchange for their brother.

When Reuben returned, he was totally horrified to find the pit empty. "What have you done!" he screamed. "Whatever am I going to do now?" He wept bitterly while his brothers got on with the business of making up an excuse for their father. They killed a young kid, took the

remaining tatters of Joseph's coat and smeared them with blood, then went to give Jacob the evidence that his favourite son had been killed by wild animals.

At the sight of the savaged coat, Jacob wept uncontrollably, beside himself with grief. He mourned Joseph day after day, and no one could comfort him.

Joseph sold into slavery

Joseph leaves his home in Hebron to go and join his brothers in the normal pastures at Shechem, but they are trying to avoid their brother so they have moved on to other meadows. Someone tells Joseph where they have gone, so he follows them to Dothan. When he is sold he is taken hundreds of miles away, down into Egypt where he works for Potiphar.

Slave traders
This illustration shows Joseph's brothers selling him to the Ishmaelite traders, also called Midianites. They are the same group of people that Gideon, one of the Judges, fought against in the Old Testament Book of Judges.

Sold!
These coins are shekels, and they are the sort of coins that Joseph's brothers were given when they sold him.

> ❖ **ABOUT THE STORY** ❖
>
> *Joseph's brothers are irritated by his strange dreams, and jealous of Jacob's favouritism. They plan to kill him, but God is on Joseph's side and his life is spared. Instead, he is sold and taken to Egypt, where the meaning of his dreams will eventually become clear.*

Joseph in Egypt

JOSEPH had been betrayed by his brothers and felt lost and terrified. He spent every minute of his uncomfortable journey wondering what would become of him and worrying about what his brothers would have told their father. When they reached Egypt, Joseph realized it was unlikely he'd ever see home again. The Ishmaelites sold Joseph as a slave to Potiphar, the captain of the Egyptian royal guard, and he found himself working in the house of Pharaoh.

Even though it felt to Joseph as though he'd been abandoned, God watched over him, keeping him safe and blessing everything he did. People soon noticed that Joseph seemed to be unusually lucky; even Potiphar realized that everything worked out well when Joseph was around, so he put him in charge of his household.

But Joseph also attracted unwelcome attention. Potiphar's wife began to fancy the young man she saw taking control of everything so well. She took great pleasure in spending her day tracking Joseph down and finding new ways to flirt with him. Joseph didn't want to have anything to do with her. "My master has been good to me. There's no way I'd go behind his back," Joseph would tell the woman firmly. "Anyway, loving another man's wife is a sin against God." But Potiphar's wife wouldn't give up. Each time Joseph said no to her, it simply made her more determined. "If sweet talk isn't working, I'll have to try something a bit more obvious," she thought to herself in the end. She waited for a quiet moment and then flung herself at Joseph, grabbing him and pulling him close to her. Struggling frantically, Joseph

wriggled free, leaving Potiphar's wife grasping a torn handful of tunic. "No one rejects me like this and gets away with it," she thought to herself in a rage. She waited until her husband came home and then began to create a terrible fuss. "Your slave broke into my room and tried to attack me," she wailed. "It was so frightening! I screamed as loud as I could and he ran off, catching his tunic on the door." Potiphar was angry and hurt. Without giving Joseph a chance to explain, he had him flung into prison.

Even locked up inside a deep, dark dungeon, God didn't desert Joseph. The prison warden knew how successful Joseph had been as Pharaoh's housekeeper, and he made

Pyramids
Ancient Egypt is probably most famous for its pyramids. These massive constructions took around 20 years to complete. Each one housed the tomb of a pharaoh, buried deep inside. The sphinx is a lion's body with a human head. This one was carved about 4000 years ago for the Pharaoh Khafre.

Royal signature
The kings of Egypt are referred to in the Bible as the Pharaohs. 'Pharaoh' originally meant the royal palace, and was only later used to mean the ruler himself. The picture signs, or hieroglyphs, shown here are the Egyptians' writing, and spell out the name of Rameses II on a tablet called a cartouche.

him responsible for taking care of the prison, giving him special rights and privileges. Two of the prisoners in Joseph's charge were also members of Pharaoh's household: his baker and his butler. One morning, Joseph found them both deep in thought, looking very puzzled. "We've each had a strange dream," they told him, "and we haven't a clue what they mean."

"Dreams come from God," Joseph said. "Tell me about them and I'll see if I can interpret them for you."

The butler went first. "I dreamt that I was looking at three bunches of grapes on a vine and I pressed them into wine for Pharaoh."

> ## But the Lord was with Joseph, and gave him steadfast love.

"Your dream means that in three days' time you will be released and will go back to your job," Joseph assured the delighted man. "I beg you, don't forget me. If it's possible for you to ask Pharaoh to pardon me, I'd be so grateful."

Then it was the baker's turn. "I dreamt that I was carrying three baskets of cakes on my head, but birds flew down and pecked away every crumb."

Joseph was troubled. "I fear your dream means that in three days Pharaoh will hang you," he said, and for three days, the men waited in agony to see what would happen.

Everything that Joseph had predicted came true. The baker was put to death, but Pharaoh restored the butler to his former job. The butler was so overjoyed that he tried to wipe all memories of the dungeon from his mind. He threw himself back into his old job and forgot about Joseph, who continued to spend his days locked up in Pharaoh's dark and damp prison.

⚜ ABOUT THE STORY ⚜

Throughout Joseph's time in Egypt, God watches over him and he soon does well. He rejects the love of Potiphar's wife, for he knows that it is a sin to love another man's wife. The woman's lies cause him to be thrown into prison but, even there, God stays with him and Joseph is well treated. Using the gift given to him by God, Joseph interprets the dreams of the butler and the baker, and his predictions come true.

Cupbearers
Not all slaves were forced to work as builders or farmers - some were given an important role in the household, and were greatly trusted by their masters. Joseph soon rose to such a position of responsibility. We do not know what his title was, but one of the highest officials was the cupbearer. His duty was to taste food and drink before serving it to the royal family, to ensure it did not contain poison. This painting shows a cupbearer serving an Egyptian prince and princess.

Pharaoh's Dream

Two years after the butler had been released from prison, Pharaoh was troubled by vivid dreams that he couldn't understand. All of his wise men offered opinions on what they meant, but Pharaoh knew they were only guessing. There seemed to be no one in the whole of his kingdom who could interpret them correctly.

It was only then that the butler remembered Joseph, and Pharaoh rushed to have him brought up from the dungeon. "I was standing by the River Nile," Pharaoh told him, "and seven fat cows came to graze at the grassy riverbank. As I watched, seven thin cows came and ate them – but the thin cows didn't get any bigger. In my second dream, I saw seven plump ears of corn being swallowed up by seven thin, shrivelled ears of corn."

The whole court waited anxiously to hear what Joseph would say. "God is warning you that there will be excellent harvests throughout Egypt for seven years, followed by seven years of devastating famine," he announced. "You should put somone in charge of stockpiling grain over the next seven seasons, otherwise your people will starve." Pharaoh knew exactly who he wanted for such a responsible task – the man before him. So Joseph went from being a captive in Pharaoh's prison to his right-hand man, dressed in the finest robes and wearing Pharaoh's ring, and he went through the country, making sure the peoples' stores were filling with grain.

After seven years, just as Joseph had predicted, the crops suddenly failed – not just in Egypt but in the lands beyond, too. Families found themselves and their animals without food and unable to grow anything in the dry ground. Joseph opened the storehouses and starving people came from far and wide for corn. Imagine Joseph's shock when one day, among the desperate people, he recognized ten of his own brothers. His only sadness was that his favourite brother, Benjamin, wasn't with them.

> " *And Pharaoh said to Joseph, 'Behold, I have set you over all the land of Egypt.'* "

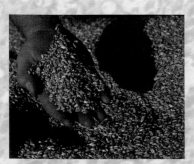

Storing grain
Joseph was responsible for storing-up grain for the famine. Severe famines have been recorded in Egypt at this time, caused by the Nile's annual floodwaters either being too low, or flooding too high. Either situation was very bad for farming.

Signet rings
This ancient Egyptian signet ring is probably like the one Pharaoh gave Joseph. Handing over the ring was a sign that Pharaoh was giving Joseph great power. Signet rings were also used to sign documents. By pressing it into clay or wax, the writing made a signature.

In the 20 years since the men had sold their brother into slavery, Joseph had changed a great deal and they had no idea who he really was. Joseph resisted the urge to hug them and instead treated the foreigners severely. He spoke to them in Egyptian, using an interpreter. "You are spies come to search out our storehouses," he accused the famished, exhausted men.

"No, we're from a starving family in Canaan," they explained. "Our youngest brother is at home with our father." Joseph pretended not to believe them and threw them in prison. After three nights, he saw them again.

"Prove that you are telling the truth," demanded Joseph. "You can go back with your corn, but one of you must stay until you bring me this youngest brother of yours."

"This is our punishment for killing Joseph," whispered Reuben, not realizing that Joseph could understand. When he saw the guilt on his brothers' faces he turned away and wept. Then he gave orders for Simeon to be bound and had every sack filled with corn, replacing their money, too.

The brothers were deeply shaken when they arrived home and found that their silver had mysteriously appeared back in their sacks. Their father was even more upset. "I lost Joseph and now I've lost Simeon," Jacob wept. "I won't let you take Benjamin or he might not come back either." But the famine lasted longer than the corn, and the family soon faced starvation again. Jacob was still determined not to let his sons return to Egypt, but when Judah promised to guard Benjamin with his life, Jacob reluctantly changed his mind. He loaded them up with gifts of exotic spices, making sure they had enough money to pay back the silver they owed.

When Joseph saw Benjamin, he wept with joy. He left the room and sent in the finest food and drink to the men. Also Joseph told his steward to fill the sacks and replace their money again, this time hiding his own silver drinking goblet in Benjamin's sack.

The brothers hadn't got very far on their return journey when Joseph sent his steward chasing after them, on the pretence of looking for the precious goblet. They were bewildered and horrified when it was found in Benjamin's sack. Back at Joseph's house they threw themselves at his mercy. "You're all free to leave," Joseph told them, "except the man in whose sack the goblet was found."

 'I am your brother Joseph, who you sold into Egypt.'

Judah knew this would break Jacob's heart. "Please let Benjamin go, or my father will die of grief," he pleaded. "Allow me to stay here in his place."

Joseph could bear it no longer. "I am your brother, Joseph, who you sold into slavery in Egypt," he told the astonished men, "and I forgive you for everything. It was all God's work. Spend the remaining years of the famine here, where I can look after everyone."

Jacob wouldn't believe that Joseph was not only alive, but lord of all Egypt under Pharaoh. But when the two men met and Jacob looked into Joseph's eyes, he knew that God had given back the son he thought was dead. "Now that I've seen you again, I can die happy," he said, thanking God. And Jacob lived out the rest of his days in Egypt.

Joseph and his brothers
When Joseph meets his brothers again for the first time in 20 years they have no idea that the grand Egyptian official in front of them is the boy they sold as a slave, and Joseph does not immediately reveal his true identity to them. The picture on the right, from a 6th-century manuscript, shows the brothers filling their sacks with grain. Joseph wears a long cloak, while his brothers are dressed in short tunics. These are not, in fact, the clothes that would have been worn in Egypt at the time of Joseph, but it is common for artists to show people wearing the clothes of the artist's time.

Moses in the Bulrushes

WHEN Joseph reached the age of 110 years old, he realized he was going to die. He called his brothers to him and promised them that God would one day return their families to Canaan - the land that the Lord had given to Abraham's descendants. But for now, the descendants of Joseph and his brothers would remain in Egypt.

Over hundreds of years their families grew and spread through the country, and they became a strong, successful people. There came a time when the Pharaoh grew worried about the huge number of powerful Israelites living in Egypt. 'Surely there are now more of these Hebrew foreigners living in our country than there are Egyptians!' he thought to himself.

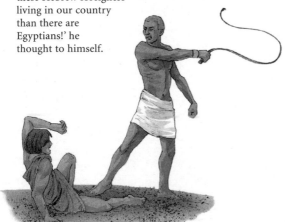

'What happens if there is a war? They might join with the enemy against us and try to take Egypt for themselves.' Pharaoh came to the conclusion that the only way to protect his people was to crush the Israelites completely. He commanded that they should all be taken as slaves and set to hard labour. It was no use anyone trying to resist Pharaoh's soldiers. Soon, groups of Israelites were to be seen digging dusty roads, ploughing up rocky fields, and being flogged when they collapsed in the baking sun. But Pharaoh wasn't satisfied. Even though he could control the Israelites' activities, he couldn't control their spirit. The more harshly they were treated, the more bitter and defiant they became. And worst of all, the number of Israelites in Egypt continued to grow! Pharaoh decided to be totally ruthless and wipe them out. He gave the order that all newborn Israelite boys should be put to death.

> 66 *Pharaoh commanded, 'Every son born to the Hebrews you shall cast into the Nile.'* 99

The terrified Israelites did everything they could to save their newborn sons. Anguished parents all over Egypt tried to hide their baby boys away or smuggle them out of the country to relatives or friends. They'd do anything to save their sons from the swords of Pharaoh's soldiers. One woman from the tribe of Levi managed to hide her baby boy in her house for three months. Every minute, she was afraid that an Egyptian would hear him crying. But as the baby grew bigger, she knew it would be impossible to keep

Finding Moses
This illustration shows Pharaoh's daughter standing on the riverbank, surrounded by her maids. In the story, the basket is covered, but here it is shown to be open, with the baby clearly visible. When illustrating a story, artists will often change details like this, to make their pictures more interesting or dramatic.

Adoption
Adoption is not common in the Old Testament. Families had other ways of dealing with the problem if parents could not have children, for example by the practice of polygamy, where a man has more than one wife. When an adoption did take place, it was more likely to be within the family.

him safe at home forever. She wove a basket out of bulrushes from the river Nile and made it watertight. Then the grief-stricken mother laid her baby in it, covered it over, and set the cradle floating among the reeds at the river's edge. The poor woman couldn't bear to leave her son without knowing what happened to him, yet she knew she was in danger if she was found nearby. So she told her daughter to stay close and watch what happened.

It wasn't long before the little girl saw a young woman coming down to the river to bathe, accompanied by many maids. "It's Pharaoh's daughter herself!" the girl realized, and watched, trembling, as the princess caught sight of the basket. Pharaoh's daughter sent a maid to fetch it, and the women all crowded round, excited to see what was inside. Gingerly, the princess began to remove the cover. Whatever could it be? Maybe someone had hidden precious jewellery, or rich spices? She was amazed to lift out of the basket a wriggling baby boy! As the baby looked up at her and began to cry, the princess's heart melted. 'This must be a Hebrew child,' she thought.

As soon as the baby's sister saw that the princess had taken pity on the baby, she plucked up her courage and approached the royal party. The little girl curtseyed and took a deep breath. "Maybe I could find an Israelite nurse to help you look after him?" she suggested. The princess thought it was an excellent idea.

The woman couldn't believe it when Pharaoh's daughter employed her to look after her own child. "I am calling him Moses," the princess said, "because it means 'to draw out' and I drew him out of the water." The princess loved Moses as if he were her own child.

Farming in Egypt
Most Israelites in Egypt were farmers. They depended on the river Nile, which flooded every year and spilt fertile soil over its banks and watered the ground.

The name of the plant
Although it is said that Moses was found among the rushes, these are more likely to have been papyrus plants, which grew in abundance beside the Nile. 'Rushes' was a word that was used as a general word for plants that grew in water.

The Burning Bush

EVEN though Moses grew up in the heart of the Egyptian royal family, he could never forget that he was an Israelite. It pained him to see that while he lived a life of luxury, all around his people suffered terribly at the hands of the Egyptians. It had become so usual to see Egyptians beating Israelite slaves that nobody took any notice. But once, Moses came across an Israelite being kicked to the ground, and suddenly he found himself rushing at the Egyptian attacker. He hit him until he was dead. Nobody was about, so Moses took the body and buried it. But next day, as he tried to split up an argument between two Israelites, one of them angrily said, "Who gave you the right to judge us? Are you going to kill us like you killed the Egyptian?" Somehow, Moses had been found out. He knew he would be in trouble if Pharaoh heard of his crime, so he fled Egypt to the land of Midian.

Moses would have been homeless if he hadn't stopped to help seven sisters trying to water their sheep. In return for his kindness, their father, Jethro, invited Moses to stay with them and also gave him work as a shepherd. Moses lived happily with Jethro's family, eventually falling in love and marrying one of Jethro's daughters, Zipporah.

Shepherding was a quiet life in comparison to the Egyptian royal household. Moses would take his flock out onto the mountain pastures with nothing but the sun and the animals for company. One day, he was deep in thought when a nearby thornbush suddenly burst into flames. After recovering from the shock, Moses went to have a closer look. He was amazed to see that although the bush was on fire, it wasn't burning up. He was even more amazed when a voice called from the flames.

> ‘I will send you to Pharaoh, that you may bring forth my people out of Egypt.’

"Moses! Moses!" Moses was terrified. "You are standing on holy ground," came the voice, "and I am the God of Abraham, Isaac and Jacob. I have seen how my people suffer in Egypt and I have heard their cries for help. I want you to go to Pharaoh

The fire of God
Usually when a bush or plant burns, the flames spread over the field, as here, and the grass catches fire, burns up and is destroyed. However, the bush Moses saw was burning in a different way. Although it was on fire, the flames did not destroy it. Moses was amazed by this unusual sight. God's presence is often symbolized by fire, which serves as a reminder of his power and holiness.

Moses's sandals
In ancient times, most poor people went barefoot, as sandals were a luxury. They were mainly worn when travelling long distances. Moses would probably have worn sandals woven from papyrus, palm leaves and grass, like the Egyptian ones here.

and rescue them. Then take them to the land I promised would be given to Abraham's descendants."

"Who am I, to be able to do all that?" he said, anxiously.

"I will be with you," replied God.

"But the people will ask me who you are," said Moses. "What shall I say?"

"I am who I am," thundered the voice. "Tell them that the God of their fathers has sent you."

"What if they don't believe me?" Moses protested.

"Throw your shepherd's crook to the ground," the voice commanded. Moses did as he was told and watched as the crook became a hissing snake. "Take hold of the snake's tail," the voice ordered. Moses forced himself to reach out his hand and the snake became his crook again.

"Now put your hand inside your shirt," it instructed. Once again, Moses did as he was told. When he pulled his hand out, he was horrified to see that his skin was covered with sores. Quickly, he thrust his hand back inside his shirt, and on drawing it out found the skin healed.

While Moses was still marvelling at these miracles, the voice spoke again. "If the people don't believe these signs, take some water from the river Nile and sprinkle it on the ground. The drops will turn into blood."

Yet Moses still had one worry – he hated speaking in public. "Take Aaron, your brother," He commanded. "He can act as your spokesperson while you show the people the signs I have sent you. Now go, and remember that I will be with you."

With a heart full of fear, Moses came down from the mountain to prepare himself for the seemingly impossible task that lay ahead.

Holy ground

This detail from a mosaic in San Vitale Church in Italy, shows Moses removing his sandals. God asked him to do so as a sign of respect, because he was walking on holy ground. In the Middle East at this time it was customary to perform religious ceremonies barefoot. This helped to keep holy places free from dirt. Moses's meeting with God took place on Mount Sinai, also called Mount Horeb. This is believed to be the mountain known today as Jebel Musa, which means Mountain of Moses.

✤ ABOUT THE STORY ✤

Although Moses was brought up at the Egyptian court, he is concerned about his people, the Israelites. He kills an Egyptian man when he sees him attacking an Israelite slave. Because of this, he has to flee from Egypt. After living as a shepherd, Moses is visited by God, who calls upon him to go to Pharaoh and rescue the Israelites from slavery. At first, Moses hesitates, but he is persuaded by God's miracles.

Moses warns Pharaoh

WHEN Moses told his father-in-law what God had instructed him to do, Jethro gave him his blessing, saying that he shouldn't delay in doing the Lord's work but leave at once. So Moses, his wife Zipporah and their sons packed up all their belongings, said goodbye to the comfort and safety of their home, and headed off towards the possible dangers lying in wait in Egypt.

God had already tried to reassure Moses by telling him that the Egyptians who wanted to kill him were now dead. But Moses was still very anxious about God's command. He grew more nervous when the Lord again appeared to him during the journey. He warned Moses that even if he performed all the miracles, Pharaoh still might not believe that he was sent by God. "Tell Pharaoh that the people of Israel are as dear to me as a first-born child," He commanded Moses. "You must warn Pharaoh that if he doesn't free my people, I will wreak a terrible vengeance."

God had told Moses' brother, Aaron, to meet Moses along the way, and the two men carefully discussed every detail of all they had to say and do. How important it was that they convinced Pharaoh! The freedom of the whole Hebrew race was resting on their shoulders, and if they failed, the Egyptian people would suffer too.

The first thing they did on reaching Egypt was to gather together the leaders of all the Israelite communities. Aaron gave a rousing speech, inspiring them with great hope and courage. And when they saw that Moses had the power to perform miracles they gasped and fell on their knees, praising God. The people realized that the Lord was truly

" *But Pharaoh said 'Who is the Lord that I should heed his voice and let Israel go?'* **"**

SEVERAL TIMES GOD IS SAID TO HAVE HARDENED PHARAOH'S HEART AND MADE HIM OBSTINATE, BUT THIS WAS NOT DONE AGAINST PHARAOH'S WILL. GOD JUST LET PHARAOH HAVE WHAT HE WANTED. ❧

The slaves suffer
Moses and Aaron had hoped to improve the lives of the Israelite slaves. However, Pharaoh was so angry at their request for freedom that he ordered the slave-masters to treat the slaves even more harshly than before. He did not care that it was the will of God that they be freed.

Symbol of life
This Egyptian symbol of life is called the *ankh*. Only kings, queens and gods were allowed to carry it. It was believed that whoever was holding the ankh had the power to give life, or take it away from others. This ankh is decorated with a dog-headed sceptre, which symbolizes power.

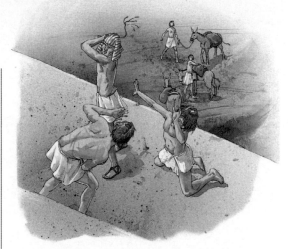

with them; He had answered their prayers and sent Moses to deliver them out of the cruel hands of the Egyptians. They were eager to follow him and do whatever he said.

After this success, Moses and Aaron felt more confident. But the most difficult task was yet to come. They had to get an audience with Pharaoh, and then tell the king of Egypt that what he was doing to the Israelites was wrong.

As they had expected, Pharaoh was outraged when the two Hebrew men dared to criticize him. "Who is this God of yours that you say has sent you?" he roared. "And even if he exists, why should I listen to him?"

"Our God has commanded all the Israelite people to travel into the desert and make a sacrifice of thanks to Him," Moses and Aaron protested. "If we don't obey, He'll strike out at everyone with His anger."

"I know nothing about your God," spat Pharaoh in a rage, "and I certainly will not set the Israelites free!" He turned to his royal guard. "Get these two out of here," he yelled. "Since they put these ridiculous ideas into the Israelites' heads, it's all the slaves can think about. Their work is getting slower and slower." As the soldiers dragged Moses and Aaron away, Pharaoh furiously commanded, "Tell all the slave-masters to stop giving the Hebrews straw to make their bricks. They'll have to go out into the fields and find straw for themselves. And if they make any fewer bricks than before, there'll be serious trouble!"

Of course, it was impossible for the Israelites to find their own straw and still make as many bricks as before. When Moses and Aaron saw how savagely the Egyptians beat them for failing at their work, they felt as if it was all their fault. "Why ever did you send me, Lord?" Moses

cried. "Ever since we spoke to Pharaoh, the people have suffered more, not less."

"Reassure the people that their God has not forgotten them," the Lord told Moses. "If I have to, I will force Pharaoh to let them go. Try once more to talk to him, and if he still refuses to obey me, wait and see what I will do. In the end, Pharaoh will be glad to see them go!"

Moses and Aaron did as God commanded. "I've told you before, I don't believe a word you say," Pharaoh scoffed. "If a god really had sent you, you'd be able to perform miracles." At this, Moses threw his crook on the ground and it became a snake. But Pharaoh wasn't impressed. He had many magicians in his court and they too threw down staffs which turned into snakes. Even though Moses' snake swallowed all the magicians' snakes, Pharaoh simply sneered. Moses was just as far away from rescuing the Israelites as ever.

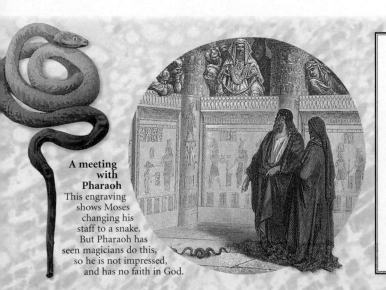

A meeting with Pharaoh
This engraving shows Moses changing his staff to a snake. But Pharaoh has seen magicians do this, so he is not impressed, and has no faith in God.

❧ ABOUT THE STORY ❧

Moses is very aware that God has made him, and his brother Aaron, responsible for the freedom of the Israelite people. Pharaoh, though, remains arrogant and refuses to believe in God. Instead of freeing the Israelites as is God's will, he makes them suffer even more. The Israelites too suffer from a lack of faith, and turn against Moses. But God reassures Moses, and he approaches Pharaoh again, but to no avail.

Plagues of Egypt

GOD saw that even a miracle wouldn't convince Pharaoh to let the Israelites go, and He knew that Pharaoh's heart was as hard as stone. The Lord told Moses and Aaron to go to the river Nile the following morning and wait for Pharaoh. As soon as Pharaoh was near, Moses drew himself up. "We were sent to you by God and you have failed to recognize Him!" Aaron thundered. "You have disobeyed His commands and refused to let the Hebrew people go. Now prepare to see how powerful the God of the Israelites really is." Moses lashed his crook down on the waters. Instantly, the river began to run red with blood. Each drop of water in every pool, lake, canal, stream and river throughout Egypt turned to blood. As the fish choked and died, the stench of rotting was everywhere, and for seven days there was no fresh water.

But Pharaoh remained unmoved. His magicians showed him that they could make water turn red through trickery, and Pharaoh ignored what Moses and Aaron had done. So God commanded the two men to strike the Nile with the sacred crook again. Straight away the bloody waters began to bubble as frogs started to hop out onto the banks. First there were hundreds, then thousands. Soon every Egyptian house was filled with leaping, croaking creatures. The Egyptians couldn't cook, eat or sleep without frogs jumping on them. Even the royal palace was overrun with the slimy creatures. Pharaoh called Moses and Aaron to him. "Tell your God to take away the frogs and I will let the Israelites go." The rejoicing men prayed to the Lord and the frogs immediately began to die. But the cheating Pharaoh told Moses that he had changed his mind, and the Israelites had to stay where they were.

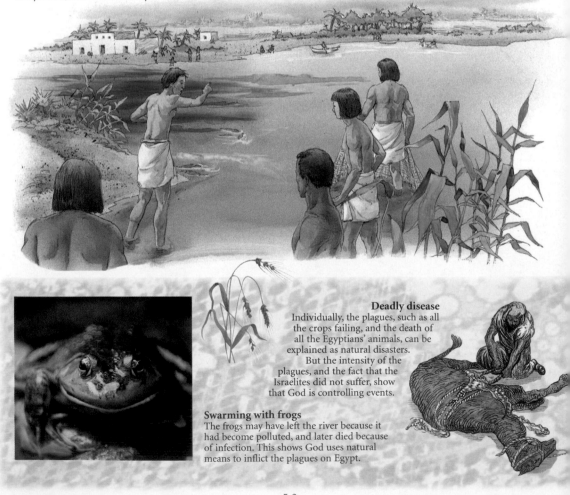

Deadly disease
Individually, the plagues, such as all the crops failing, and the death of all the Egyptians' animals, can be explained as natural disasters. But the intensity of the plagues, and the fact that the Israelites did not suffer, show that God is controlling events.

Swarming with frogs
The frogs may have left the river because it had become polluted, and later died because of infection. This shows God uses natural means to inflict the plagues on Egypt.

At this, God commanded the two men to hit the earth with Moses' crook. Each tiny speck of dust turned into a squirming maggot – it looked as if the whole of the ground was moving! Maggots wriggled over every man, woman and animal, and as fast as they brushed them off, they found more crawling over their skin.

Then God sent a plague of flies. "But you'll see that there will be no insects where the Israelites live," they told Pharaoh. Almost before they had finished speaking, huge humming clouds of flies came swarming through the air, settling in their millions on the Egyptian households without going anywhere near a single Israelite.

The very next day, the Egyptian farmers found all their animals struck down with a mysterious disease. They could do nothing but watch as every cow, sheep and camel died, while the animals belonging to the Israelites remained healthy. But this only infuriated Pharaoh, and made him determined not to give in to the Israelites.

God told Moses to take two handfuls of soot and scatter it into the wind. The breeze carried it far and wide, and people found their skin breaking out into hideous sores. Then the two men sent a hailstorm so fierce that anything caught outside would die. The Lord hurled down bolts of thunder and flashes of lightning, and pelted the Egyptians with piercing hailstones. Pharaoh said that the Israelites could leave, and the sun broke through the clouds.

But the sunshine did not last long. Pharaoh told Moses and Aaron that he had once more lied to them, and the skies darkened again the very same day. A strange rustling noise blew towards Egypt on the wind, and the people realized that it was the wings of swarms of locusts. Millions of the insects fell on the earth like a black carpet, stripping the soil bare by devouring every remaining leaf and shoot. Utter destruction faced the whole country and Pharaoh once again tried to compromise with Moses and Aaron. He promised to let all the male Israelites go free - but it wasn't enough. Moses raised his hand and Egypt

❝ And the locusts came up over the whole land of Egypt ❞

suddenly found itself in darkness. God had blotted out the Sun, leaving the Egyptians in inky blackness.

After three days, Pharaoh could take it no longer. "Go!" he ordered Moses and Aaron. "And take every last Israelite with you! But I say this on one condition – they have to leave all their flocks and herds behind."

"You know we cannot agree to that," Moses answered.

Pharaoh gripped the arms of his throne so hard that his knuckles turned white. "Then the Israelites will remain as slaves in Egypt forever," he hissed "and if you ever dare to enter my presence again, you will be put to death."

❧ ABOUT THE STORY ❧

God brings about the plagues to show His supreme power. The Egyptians worshipped many gods of their own. By destroying the symbols of the Egyptian gods, God shows He is more powerful. However, despite the plagues, Pharaoh refuses to obey God's will.

In the dark
Some people say that the darkness was caused by an eclipse, but this could not last three days. It is more likely that earth washed down by the storms dried into dust. This was whirled up into a dust-storm by a strong wind that stopped the sun getting through.

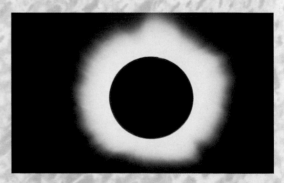

The Passover

How arrogant Pharaoh was! The Egyptians traditionally believed that their Pharaoh was a god, and he expected to be treated as one. He certainly wasn't used to people telling him his laws were wrong and defying his orders. No matter how much suffering was inflicted on his people, Pharaoh couldn't bring himself to acknowledge the existence of the Hebrew God - let alone admit that the Lord was far mightier than he was. Moses and Aaron had correctly predicted plagues nine times, and even Pharaoh's counsellors had been convinced. "Don't you understand that Egypt is ruined?" they had pleaded in frustration with Pharaoh. "You must let the Israelites go to worship their God!" But Pharaoh shut himself away in his palace, closing his eyes to his people's wretchedness and blocking his ears to their cries.

After Pharaoh's final threat, God again spoke to Moses. "I will bring one last plague upon Pharaoh and his country. It will be so terrible that he will end up begging the Israelites to leave Egypt. Tonight, all first-born children will die – from the family of Pharaoh himself to the very poorest household. I will even kill first-born animals. Through the whole of Egypt, only the Israelites will be spared from grief. This is what you are to tell them to do. Each Hebrew household must kill a male lamb at sunset and sprinkle some of its blood around the front door. The lamb is then to be roasted and eaten with bitter herbs and flat bread, and any left overs must be burnt. The people must hurry and go to bed early. Tell them to lock themselves inside their houses and, whatever happens, not

66 *'For I will pass through the land of Egypt and I will smite all the first born.'* 99

Holy book
This is an illuminated page of a Jewish book called the Haggadah. Parts of the book are read or recited during the Passover feast. The Haggadah contains stories, poems and rituals that are significant to the Jewish religion, including sections of the Torah. The Torah is the name given to the first five books of the Old Testament in the Bible, the most important part of Jewish scriptures.

Ruling pharaoh
Rameses II is believed to have been the ruling Pharaoh at the time of the Passover. This picture shows part of a colossal statue of him on a huge temple cut into the rocks at Abu Simbel in Nubia. When the Aswan Dam was built in the 1960s, the whole temple had to be taken down and moved to a new location so it would not be flooded.

to go outside until morning. For at midnight I will pass over the whole land and slay the first-born child in every household that isn't marked with blood. This night will be known as the Passover and you must remember it each year as a holy festival." With dread and fear in his heart, Moses hastened to call the Israelite leaders together and give them God's instructions.

The next day, it wasn't the sun that woke the land of Egypt – it was the sound of screaming. As each family found their beloved first-born child lying dead in their bed, they sent up heartbroken cries that tore the air, until it seemed as if the whole of Egypt was wailing. Somebody had died in every household from the royal palace to the darkest prison – except for the homes of the Israelites.

Even before the dawn had fully broken, Moses and Aaron were summoned to see Pharaoh. They found the once-proud king completely broken by grief. His eyes were swollen with weeping, his face wrenched into haggard lines of pain, and his shoulders slumped with the heaviness of utter misery. "Leave my land," he groaned in agony, barely able to speak. "Take whatever you want and go." Moses and Aaron knew that, this time, Pharaoh's words came from the heart. Without further hesitation, they turned to go and spread the good news to the Israelites. But the thin crackle of Pharaoh's voice stopped them. "Ask the Lord to bless me, too," he whispered.

And so it was that, after 430 years of slavery, the Israelites finally left Egypt. The Egyptians hurried them away with presents of gold, silver, fine materials and other expensive gifts. And led by Moses, over six hundred thousand men, women and children set off on foot on their long journey into the wilderness.

Passover today

Today, Jewish families hold a feast to remember the Passover as God commanded. They gather together to eat specially prepared food that symbolizes the sufferings of the Israelites in Egypt. The meal begins after dark and before any food is eaten, the youngest child asks the oldest family member to retell the story of the Passover.

Hyssop

Hyssop, the name given to the leaves of the marjoram plant, was a common symbol of purity. Moses told the Israelites to use a bunch of hyssop to smear the lamb's blood around their doors on the night of the Passover.

❧ ABOUT THE STORY ❧

Although many people, even in Pharaoh's household, are convinced about the existence of God, Pharaoh remains arrogant. It is only when God sends the final plague that Pharaoh realises Moses is right. Pharaoh abandons his pride, releases the Israelites and asks for God's blessing. The Passover is so called because God 'passed over' the houses of the Israelites, meaning He spared them from the plague.

Crossing the Red Sea

THE minute the Israelites had gone, Pharaoh regretted his decision. The rate at which grand buildings and beautiful monuments were going up slowed right down as soon as the slave labour departed. Each time Pharaoh caught sight of a deserted building site he was reminded that he had lost some of his power. He imagined his former slaves travelling further out of his grasp, and he became more and more resentful. After several days of being tormented by his own thoughts, Pharaoh finally called a meeting of his counsellors. "We should never have let the Hebrews go!" he raged. "I want as many troops as possible sent after them. You must find the Israelites and bring them back!"

Meanwhile, the Israelites were making good progress through the desert, helped by God. By day a whirling column of cloud guided them and by night a blazing pillar of flame lit the way.

The Israelites were at first puzzled when they looked back and saw a cloud of dust coming towards them at top speed. Then, as they recognized the glints of golden armour in the sun, and heard the noise of thundering hooves, panic spread among them. "Did you bring us here to die!" they shrieked at Moses. "It would have been better to live in slavery under the Egyptians than die here!"

"Have faith in the Lord who brought you here," he said.

Moses fell silent, believing wholeheartedly that God would answer his prayer. He listened as the people's cries changed from terror to wonderment. The column of cloud had moved behind them, smothering the Egyptians in darkness so they could not see where they were going.

> ❝ *The Lord drove the sea back and made the sea dry land and the waters were divided.* ❞

Then God told Moses to stretch out his hand towards the Red Sea ahead of them. At once, a mighty gale blew up from the east. Moses commanded the Israelites to press forward. Though no one dared protest to Moses a second time, each person knew that they were heading straight for the ocean. Surely they would all be drowned! But when they drew nearer, the Israelites could hardly believe their eyes. The wind had driven back the waters, leaving a path of dry land through the waves. They walked all night long, with walls of water towering over them on either side.

In the morning, when every last Israelite had crossed safely, Moses turned and looked back. The Egyptians had tried to follow them across the ocean floor, but the wheels of their chariots had sunk into the mud, along with their horses and the soldiers. In the chaos, they had become very afraid. "Run! Run! God must truly be with the Israelites!" some of them were yelling.

Moses stretched out his hand once more. Instantly, the walls of water came roaring down on the Egyptians. When the tide at last settled, it was as if the desperate men and all their equipment had never been there.

Weeping with relief and overcome with gratitude, the Hebrew people threw themselves to the ground, giving thanks to God. Then Moses' sister Miriam took up her tambourine to sing God's praises – after over 400 years the Israelites were on their way to their Promised Land.

Crossing the Red Sea
No one knows exactly where Moses crossed the Red Sea. We know the Israelites went from Rameses to Succoth. After this, their route, in blue, may have crossed the Reed Sea. The green route shows they may have crossed the Bitter Lake. Finally, the mauve route shows a journey along the Great Sea.

Chariots
The Egyptians' horse-drawn chariots would have been very light, made mainly of wood and leather, with a few bronze or iron fittings. The chariots were mostly open at the back, and had hooks or racks on the outside to hold weapons.

❧ ABOUT THE STORY ❧

By parting the waters of the Red Sea for them, God shows the Israelites that He intends to free them from slavery. Under the watchful gaze of God's chosen leader Moses, He guides them safely out of Egypt and sets them on the long journey towards the Promised Land.

Poetry in the Old Testament

Poetry and song played an important part in people's lives at the time of the Old Testament. Poetry would have been recited aloud and would generally have been accompanied by music, so the difference between a poem and a song was not as marked as it is for us today. Songs were sung by all kinds of people, for all kinds of reasons and at many different times.

People who worked at particular occupations probably had special songs, for example, the 'Song of the Well' (Numbers 21:17–18) might have been sung by people drawing water from a well, or by people actually digging the well. Another mention of songs connected to occupations occurs in Isaiah 16:10, where there is a description of singing in the vineyards while making wine.

Songs were also used on special occasions, such as when people arrived or departed. When Jacob tries to steal away from Laban's house without his uncle's knowledge, Laban is angry that he was not given the opportunity to send his nephew away with songs and music, as was the custom (Genesis 31:27). Songs of celebration were sung at weddings, and laments were sung for the dead.

Songs were not usually heard as voices alone; they were nearly always accompanied by instruments. The main purpose of

instruments in the Old Testament appears to be to accompany songs. The Hebrew language is very rhythmic so even passages of the Old Testament which are not really poetry can sound like poems, especially if they are part of someone's speech.

The poetry in the Old Testament does not rhyme, but it does use other devices common to all poetry, such as similes (where something is likened to something else, such as 'they went down into the depths like a stone'), metaphors (where something is described as if it were something else, 'the earth swallowed them')

Miriam's song

After the Israelites have crossed the Red Sea, Moses' sister Miriam, raises a tambourine and begins to dance. All the other women join her in the dance, and Miriam sings a song of praise to God. The words of her song (on the opposite page) tell of the Israelites' escape from Egypt and the crossing of the Red Sea.

THIS SHOWS AN ILLUMINATED, OR ORNATELY DECORATED, SONG. THIS OFTEN HAPPENED WITH RELIGIOUS SONGS.

and alliteration (where several words close to each other begin with the same letter, like 'your people pass' where the 'p' is repeated).

The use of imagery (visually descriptive language) is abundant in the poetry of the Old Testament. It draws on the universe, including the stars, the Moon and the Sun, on nature, including the seasons, the weather and the sea, and on the activities of the countryside, such as shepherding, harvest time and wine making. However, the inspiration behind all the songs and poetry in the Old Testament is the love and worship of God.

ᴥ THE SONG OF MIRIAM ᴥ

I will sing to the Lord for He has triumphed gloriously;
the horse and his rider He has thrown into the sea.
The Lord is my strength and my song,
and He has become my salvation;
this is my God, and I will praise Him,
my father's God and I will exalt Him.
The Lord is a man of war;
the Lord is His name.

Pharaoh's chariots and his host He cast into the sea;
and his picked officers are sunk in the Red Sea.
The floods covered them;
they went down into the depths like a stone.
Thy right hand, O Lord, glorious in power,
thy right hand, O Lord, shatters the enemy.
In the greatness of thy majesty thou overthrowest thy adversaries;
thou sendest forth thy fury, it consumes them like stubble.
At the blast of thy nostrils the waters piled up,
the floods stood up in a heap;
the deeps congealed in the heart of the sea.
The enemy said, "I will pursue, I will overtake,
I will divide the spoil; my desire shall have its fill of them.
I will draw my sword, my hand shall destroy them."
Thou didst blow with thy wind, the sea covered them;
they sank as lead in the mighty waters.

Who is like thee, O Lord, among the gods?
Who is like thee – majestic in holiness, terrible in glorious deeds, doing wonders?
Thou didst stretch out your right hand, the earth swallowed them.

Thou hast led in thy steadfast love the people whom thou hast redeemed,
thou hast guided them by thy strength to thy holy abode.
The peoples have heard, they tremble;
pangs have seized on the inhabitants of Philistia.
The chiefs of Edom will be terrified,
the leaders of Moab will be seized with trembling,
the people of Canaan will melt away;
terror and dread will fall upon them.
By the power of your arm they will be as still as a stone,
until your people pass by, O Lord,
until the people you bought pass by.
You will bring them in and plant them
on the mountain of your inheritance,
the place, O Lord, you made for your dwelling,
the sanctuary, O Lord, your hands established.
The Lord will reign for ever and ever.

Judaism and the Old Testament

The books of the Old Testament form the Scriptures, or sacred writings, of the Jewish people. They tell the story of their ancestors, the Israelites, or Hebrews. To Jews, the most important part of the Old Testament is the first five books: Genesis, Exodus, Leviticus, Numbers and Deuteronomy. These five books are called the Torah, which means 'teaching'. The Torah contains stories, poetry, prayers and laws which teach people about God, and how they can live their lives according to His will. Of particular importance are God's covenant with Abraham, and the laws God reveals to His people through Moses.

Jewish people go to worship in the synagogue on the Sabbath, which, for them, is Saturday. Parts of the Torah are read aloud each Sabbath, by a rabbi or by another member of the congregation. After a year, the whole Torah has been read and a celebration called Simcha Torah takes place. People hold the scrolls on which the Torah is written high above their heads, and dance in a procession around the synagogue. At the next reading, the Torah is begun all over again.

Many Jewish festivals commemorate events from the Bible. For example, the Festival of the Passover, which is celebrated with a special meal, reminds Jews of how God sent a plague to kill all first-born babies, except those in the homes of the Israelites, which He 'passed over'. The festival Yom Kippur is a solemn day of fasting and prayer. In the Bible, a goat was sent into the wilderness as a sacrifice. During the festival of Succoth, also known as the Feast of Tabernacles, people camp in tents to remember the Israelites' years of wandering in the wilderness.

The Star of David
This is used as a Jewish and Israeli symbol. David was an Israelite king who captured Jerusalem and made it his capital city.

ABRAHAM   SARAH

ISAAC   REBEKAH

ESAU   JACOB   LEAH   RACHEL   ZILPAH   BILHAH

REUBEN SIMEON LEVI JUDAH ISAACHAR ZEBULUN DINAH JOSEPH BENJAMIN GAD ASHER DAN NAPHTALI

Patriarch's family tree
In the Bible, Abraham is the first great leader of the Israelites. At his death, the leadership passes to his son, Isaac, to Isaac's son, Jacob and finally to Joseph. Abraham, Isaac, Jacob and Joseph are known as the Patriarchs, meaning the male heads of a family. Jacob's other sons were also thought of as Patriarchs, and were the forefathers of the twelve tribes of Israel.

TIMELINE 2200BC TO 1400BC

Abraham, who was to become the first father of the Israelites, was born.

ANIMALS PREPARED FOR SACRIFICE

2200BC

ISAAC MEETS REBEKAH

Abraham's sons, Ishmael and Isaac, are born.

2100BC

Jacob, father of the twelve tribes of Israel, is born.

On his way to Haran Jacob sees a vision, sent by God, of a stairway to heaven, and God's covenant is renewed with Jacob.

Jacob gets married and his sons, including Joseph, are born.

Joseph is sold to traders and taken to Egypt, where he finds favour with Pharaoh.

2000BC

Jacob and his family move to Egypt to live with Joseph.

Over the years the Israelites increase in number. Later pharaohs make them slaves to protect their power.

JACOB AND ESAU ARE REUNITED

1900BC   18

The Origins of the Bible

The words of the earliest books of the Old Testament were passed down by word of mouth before they were written down in Hebrew. The first five books may have been written as early as 1400BC, and the latest books not until around 450BC. It took almost a thousand years for the whole Old Testament to be written down.

The books of the Bible were written by many different authors, but not all can be identified. Some may have had several authors, or may have been altered by other people. The first five books of the Bible are traditionally believed to have been written by Moses and are sometimes called The Five Books of Moses. There are passages which could not have written, such as the account of his death.

The Old Testament in most Christian Bibles is divided into four sections: the Pentateuch (the first five books); the Historical Books (the following 12); Poetry and Wisdom (the next five) and Prophets (the last 17). The books in the Jewish Bible are arranged differently, putting the five books of the Pentateuch, what the Jews call the law, or Torah, first. This is followed by the books of Joshua and Judges, both books of Samuel and Kings, Isaiah, Jeremiah and Ezekiel with the minor prophets. The Jewish people call this section the Naviim. Finally come the Writings, the Kethubim, which includes the remainder of the books, including Psalms, Proverbs, and the books of Ruth and Daniel.

The Jewish Talmud
This contains the Mishnah, the oral law of the Jews.

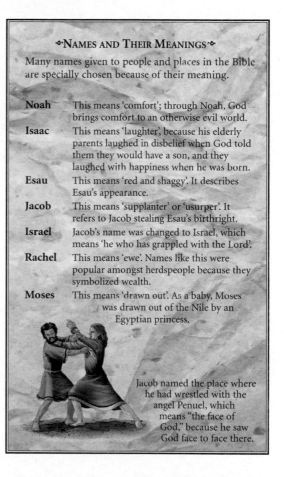

❧ NAMES AND THEIR MEANINGS ❧

Many names given to people and places in the Bible are specially chosen because of their meaning.

Noah — This means 'comfort'; through Noah, God brings comfort to an otherwise evil world.

Isaac — This means 'laughter', because his elderly parents laughed in disbelief when God told them they would have a son, and they laughed with happiness when he was born.

Esau — This means 'red and shaggy'. It describes Esau's appearance.

Jacob — This means 'supplanter' or 'usurper'. It refers to Jacob stealing Esau's birthright.

Israel — Jacob's name was changed to Israel, which means 'he who has grappled with the Lord'.

Rachel — This means 'ewe'. Names like this were popular amongst herdspeople because they symbolized wealth.

Moses — This means 'drawn out'. As a baby, Moses was drawn out of the Nile by an Egyptian princess.

Jacob named the place where he had wrestled with the angel Penuel, which means "the face of God," because he saw God face to face there.

THE PYRAMIDS WOULD HAVE LOOMED OVER THE ISRAELITES AS THEY WORKED FOR PHARAOH

THE EGYPTIANS MAKE LIFE VERY HARD FOR THE ISRAELITES

1700BC

Moses is born, and is rescued from the Nile by an Egyptian princess.

Moses kills an Egyptian, and flees to exile in a distant land called Midian.

Moses sees the burning bush, and hears God's command to return to Egypt and free the Israelites.

1600BC

After over 400 years as slaves, Moses leads the Israelites out of Egypt to the Promised Land.

MOSES COMMANDS THE RED SEA

1500BC

1400BC

Glossary

altar
An altar is a table or flat-topped block used as the focus for a religious ritual. In the Old Testament, altars were mainly used for making sacrifices or offerings to God. At the time of the Patriarchs, anyone could build an altar, but later only priests were allowed to do this.

ark
The word "ark" means "box" or "chest" in Hebrew. The same word is used in the Bible for Noah's Ark and the basket in which the baby Moses is found. Both uses represent a safe place provided by God.

birthright
The birthright was a father's special blessing to his oldest son. This gave the son leadership over his brothers, but also the responsibility of taking care of the family after his father's death.

Canaan
The area east of the Mediterranean, in what is modern Israel and Palestine. The area got its name from Canaan, son of Noah, who was the ancestor of the tribes that lived there.

covenant
A promise where God enters into a special relationship with His people. He promised His protection and the land of Canaan to Abraham and his descendants if they would be faithful to him. This idea is summed up in the words of Jeremiah 31:33; "I will be their God, and they will be my people." The main covenants in the Old Testament are with Abraham and Moses. In the New Testament, the main covenant is with all God's people, sealed with the death of Jesus on the cross.

curse
When God announces a curse it is a judgment on a person's sin. When people spoke curses to try and hurt someone they believed in the power of the curses, they really thought that they could make something happen. They also thought that the more powerful the person that said the curse, the more powerful the curse would be.

dowry
A gift given by a man to his future father-in-law before his marriage to compensate the father for the loss of his daughter.

Exodus
This is the name given to the journey that the Israelites made from Egypt to the promised land. "Exodus" itself means "going out", which describes how the Israelites left Egypt.

Fall of Man
This means peoples' first disobedience to God. Adam and Eve lived in Paradise with God with no sin to spoil their lives. When they listened to the serpent instead of God, and ate the Fruit from the Tree of the Knowledge of Good and Evil, they "fell" from the sight and blessing of God.

festival
Festivals were times of great rejoicing and feasting, giving thanks to God for harvests and occasions for remembering great events in Israel's history.

Grace
The "grace" of God is the fact that God loves all the men and women that he created even though no one on earth is completely without sin.

Israelite
The nation that descended from Jacob, who was renamed Israel after wrestling all night with an angel by the river Jabbok. The new name, which means "he who has wrestled with the Lord", was a sign that God was still with him.

miracle
These are mighty works, performed through the power of God. Moses himself performed miracles, the most famous of which is the parting of the Red Sea. The most important miracle to Christianity is the resurrection of Jesus after he was crucified.

Passover
Passover commemorates the night that God killed all the first born children of Egypt to make Pharaoh release the Israelites, but he "passed over" the homes of the Israelites, leaving them unharmed. This festival is remembered with a meal of lamb and bread made without yeast.

Patriarch
The four Patriarchs in the Old Testament are Abraham, Isaac, Jacob and Joseph. They are the male heads of the family, those with whom God made or renewed his covenant.

sacrifice
An offering made to God as a way for a man to give God something that belongs to him. Only the best can be offered to God, the first born lambs, or the best wheat. Sacrifices are not a person's attempt to earn favour from God, but a way to make peace with Him.

sin
Sin is seen as lots of different things in the Bible. Mainly it is a rebellion against God, but it is also described as not doing what one is supposed to do.

Temptation
The fact that God allows his people to be tested by temptation shows the worth of the love people feel for God. Every test that people go through strengthens believe in and love of God. Christians are told to be always on their guard against temptation, but they are also told that God will provide the power to endure it, and that temptation need never become too great to bear.

Index